822.33 TEM

KT-461-872

YORK NOTES

THE TEMPEST

WILLIAM SHAKESPEARE

NOTES BY LORETO TODD

City and Islington College

SFC14825

 Longman

 York Press

CITY AND ISLINGTON
SIXTH FORM COLLEGE
283 - 309 GOSWELL ROAD
LONDON
EC1
TEL 020 7520 0652

Exterior picture of the Globe Theatre reproduced by permission of the
Raymond Mander and Joe Mitchenson Theatre Collection
Reconstruction of the Globe Theatre interior reprinted from Hodges;
'The Globe Restored' (1968) by permission of Oxford University Press

The right of Loreto Todd to be identified as Author
of this Work has been asserted by her in accordance with the
Copyright, Designs and Patents Act 1988

YORK PRESS
322 Old Brompton Road, London SW5 9JH

PEARSON EDUCATION LIMITED
Edinburgh Gate, Harlow,
Essex CM20 2JE, United Kingdom
Associated companies, branches and representatives throughout the world

© Librairie du Liban *Publishers* 1998, 2003

All rights reserved. No part of this publication may be reproduced, stored
in a retrieval system, or transmitted in any form or by any means, electronic,
mechanical, photocopying, recording, or otherwise, without either the prior
written permission of the Publishers or a licence permitting restricted copying
in the United Kingdom issued by the Copyright Licensing Agency Ltd,
90 Tottenham Court Road, London W1T 4LP

First published 1998
This new and fully revised edition first published 2003
Eighth impression 2010

ISBN: 978-0-582-78437-6

Designed by Michelle Cannatella
Typeset by Land & Unwin (Data Sciences), Bugbrooke, Northamptonshire
Produced by Pearson Education Asia Limited, Hong Kong

CONTENTS

SFC14825
822·33 TEM
REFERENCE

PART FIVE
BACKGROUND

PART ONE

INTRODUCTION

HOW TO STUDY A PLAY

Studying on your own requires self-discipline and a carefully thought-out work plan in order to be effective.

- Drama is a special kind of writing (the technical term is '**genre**') because it needs a performance in the theatre to arrive at a full interpretation of its meaning. Try to imagine that you are a member of the audience when reading the play. Think about how it could be presented on the stage, not just about the words on the page.

- Drama is always about conflict of some sort (which may be below the surface). Identify the conflicts in the play and you will be close to identifying the large ideas or themes which bind all the parts together.

- Make careful notes on themes, character, **plot** and any **sub-plots** of the play.

- Why do you like or dislike the characters in the play? How do your feelings towards them develop and change?

- Playwrights find non-realistic ways of allowing an audience to see into the minds and motives of their characters, for example soliloquy, aside or music. Consider how such dramatic devices are used in the play you are studying.

- Think of the playwright writing the play. Why were these particular arrangements of events, characters and speeches chosen?

- Cite exact sources for all quotations, whether from the text itself or from critical commentaries. Wherever possible find your own examples from the play to back up your opinions.

- Where appropriate, comment in detail on the language of the passage you have quoted.

- Always express your ideas in your own words.

These York Notes offer an introduction to *The Tempest* and cannot substitute for close reading of the text and the study of secondary sources.

> **CONTEXT**
>
> The similarities between drama and religious ritual have been noted since classical Greek times. In both, the chief performers are distanced from the audience; the participation of the audience is largely passive; and a certain number of conventions, such as a sermon or a soliloquy, have become established.

READING *THE TEMPEST*

THE NATURE OF THE PLAY

The Tempest is, at one level, a fairy tale complete with magical occurrences, suspension of the laws of nature and a happy ending, but it is much more than this. It attempts to examine the connection between suffering and purification, the supposed contrast between civilised and uncivilised people, and to illustrate, albeit briefly, the results of colonialism. The play deals with a number of serious themes but the seriousness is not allowed to cause disquiet in the audience. In spite of threats of death and disorder, the play ends on a note of triumph. The older generations have found reconciliation, and the younger ones love; Ariel has been released from his bondage and Caliban is once again master of his island.

DRAMATIC UNITIES

In *The Tempest*, Shakespeare adheres fairly closely to what scholars have called the 'classical unities of time, place and action'. These **unities** are based on conventions established by writers of classical Greek drama.

The unity of time implied that the length of time taken by the **action** in a play should correspond approximately to the length of time taken to perform the play. Such a correspondence was hard to maintain and so it was permissible for the imaginary action to last for a maximum of twenty-four hours. *The Tempest* can be performed in about two hours whereas its action can be calculated to span just under four. In the play, Shakespeare draws the audience's attention to the time at which certain actions occur (see I.2.238–41, V.1.3–5 and V.1.185–6).

The second unity, the unity of place, required that the scene should remain unchanged throughout the play. In *The Tempest* the entire action, with the exception of the first scene, is confined to the island.

The third unity, the unity of action, prescribed that a play which adhered to the classical unities should have only one **plot** and that

---

CONTEXT

Although fairy tales are considered appropriate for children's entertainment, they are often cruel: Hansel and Gretel are abandoned; Snow White's murder is arranged by her stepmother; and little Red Riding Hood's grandmother is eaten by a wolf.

QUESTION

To what extent does Shakespeare's adherence to the classical unities of time, place and action contribute to the structural cohesion of *The Tempest*?

---

all other incidents in the play should be subordinated to it. In *The Tempest* the main plot revolves around Prospero's efforts to regain his dukedom and to undo the evil which had been perpetrated against him and his daughter, Miranda.

It is impossible to say why Shakespeare chose to observe the unities in *The Tempest* when he was largely indifferent to them in his other plays. Some **critics** have suggested that Shakespeare knew this was his last play and wanted to show that he could adhere to the classical unities when he chose. There may be some truth in this view, but it is also possible that Shakespeare simply wished to concentrate the audience's attention on the theme of reconciliation which features prominently in the play and that he found the classical unities contributed to the clarity of his presentation. Whatever his reason for observing the unities in *The Tempest*, Shakespeare was, in this play, preoccupied by the interrelated themes of sin, repentance and reconciliation, themes that Prospero directly addresses in the final scene (see V.1.25–30).

The love and harmony between Ferdinand and Miranda compensate for the quarrel and discord that separated their fathers. Because the play concentrates on evil redeemed rather than on the unhappy results of human weaknesses that are explored in such plays as *Macbeth* and *King Lear*, the setting and the behaviour are chosen more for their ability to emphasise the themes rather than for strict, naturalistic accuracy. The location of the island, for example, is never exactly specified. We are told that it is in the Mediterranean, some miles from the coast, but its exact location is less important than its ability to suggest mystery, romance and the opportunity to be alone with one's innermost thoughts. The strangeness of the island, which is at one and the same time a tropical paradise and a place where we hear of wild bulls and lions, bogs and fens, is a suitable setting for the exercise of magical charms, charms that can invoke a tempest, purge a king's guilt and allow goodness to defeat evil.

CHECK THE NET

Search for other literary texts where the protagonists are stranded on an island, for example *Robinson Crusoe, Gulliver's Travels*. Examine how other writers have used isolation as a vehicle for character development.

In *The Tempest*, as in his other plays, Shakespeare's use of ejaculations, oaths and references to God is conventionalised. On 27 May 1606 a statute was passed to prevent swearing in plays.

According to the statute, one could be fined up to £10 (a great deal of money in the seventeenth century) for profane use of the name of God, of Jesus Christ, of the Holy Ghost or of the Trinity. *The Tempest* was written after this statute was passed and so we find that Christian references are minimised, although there are many allusions to the gods of classical mythology (see, for example, I.2.201–6).

THE NATURE OF TRAGICOMEDY

Shakespearean comedies usually treat the happier aspects of life such as love and marriage, often, as in *The Tempest*, making lavish use of music and singing. Frequently there are two levels in the comedy, one involving the love interests of courtly characters, in this case Ferdinand and Miranda, and another dealing with the humorous behaviour of less elevated personalities, such as Trinculo and Stephano. Tragedies, however, deal with the harsher side of life, with the trials and eventual death of an important person. Often the hero's fall from happiness is due to a weakness in his character, a weakness such as the overweening ambition of Macbeth or the uncontrolled jealousy of Othello.

In *The Tempest* we have a combination of the two types of play. Love is a central theme, as it is in such comedies as *Twelfth Night* and *As You Like It*; music is extremely important and the words of some of Ariel's songs are an integral part of the dialogue (see, for example, I.2.397–405); and yet the audience is also made aware of the less joyful possibilities of life. They are shown that evil exists. There are the seeds of possible disaster in Prospero's overthrow, in Caliban's attempt to rape Miranda, in the treatment of Caliban and Ariel, and in the **plots** to murder Prospero and Alonso. These seeds of doom are not allowed to develop, however, and the play ends with the reconciliation of the major characters and with the suggestion that the love between Miranda and Ferdinand has helped to compensate for the strife between their fathers.

Prose is sometimes used for comic episodes (see, for example, IV.1.194–254) whereas **blank verse** is the usual medium for more serious interaction. By alternating between prose and verse Shakespeare can emphasise differences in language and behaviour

> **CONTEXT**
>
> In Act II, Scene IV of the play *Le Bourgeois Gentilhomme* by Molière (1622–73), the main character is told that verse and prose are the only two forms of self-expression. He is delighted to think that for forty-odd years he has been speaking 'prose' without knowing it! Literary prose is not, however, as spontaneous as normal speech acts, and even the jocular speech in *The Tempest* has both coherence and structural relevance to the plot.

while implying the essential similarity between the needs and urges of all his characters, and stressing, at the same time, the common humanity they share with their audience.

A NOTE ON MASQUES IN THE TEXT

Masques were stylised dramas incorporating poetic dialogue, music and dancing, and often making lavish use of costumes, scenery and mechanical devices. They began as costume balls designed around a theme, frequently a classical one. Invited performers, often wearing exotic costumes and masks, would dance before their royal host and guests. After their act, the players would invite the spectators to join in. Masques were performed at court in the reign of Henry VIII (1509–47), but they reached the height of their popularity as court entertainments in the reigns of Elizabeth (1558–1603) and James I (1603–25). Typically, masques were occasions for revelling. They were performed as part of a programme of festive events at Christmas and Easter or to celebrate a wedding. The masque usually began in the evening, and often continued late into the night or the early morning. After the presentation, the entertainment often ended with a banquet. Shakespeare provides some evidence of this type of entertainment in *Romeo and Juliet*. Romeo and his friends gatecrash the Capulets' party in a group of masquers, and Romeo meets Juliet at the dance that takes place afterwards.

Over the period of their popularity, certain conventions developed in the writing and production of masques and these can be observed in the short masque that occurs in IV.1.60–138 of *The Tempest*. Masques almost always dealt with classical or mythological subject matter; the characters were often gods and goddesses or personifications of abstract qualities such as grace or peace; they were often composed to celebrate a marriage, and so married bliss was a widely used theme; they were normally shorter than the more usual drama of the time; they frequently used rhyming couplets; and they made lavish use of music and costumes. We have no exact modern equivalent but we might think of them as a combination of the style and opulence of an opera and a ballet.

Occasionally, a dramatist did not use speech in the masque but employed **mime**, music, costumes and moving scenery to entertain

CHECK THE BOOK

Edgar Allan Poe (1809–49) was clearly influenced by *The Tempest* in his story 'The Masque of the Red Death'. He describes how, when a plague is affecting the country, Prince Prospero invites his friends to come to his isolated castle to enjoy themselves until the plague is over. As part of the entertainment, he plans a masked ball. You might like to consider the elements from the play that Poe incorporates into his story.

CHECK THE BOOK

Read the masque scenes carefully to see how Shakespeare integrates them into the dramatic action.

the audience. The banquet episode in III.3.18–52 can be regarded as a miming masque of this type. A third type of masque, often referred to as an 'antimasque', also developed in the seventeenth century. This was usually a contrasting interlude or prelude to the main masque and involved grotesque costumes and vigorous dancing. In *The Tempest*, Stephano, Trinculo and Caliban perform a function similar to the antimasque in Act IV, Scene 1.

Shakespeare's use of masques is not confined to *The Tempest*, but the appearance of three different kinds of masque in the one play may indicate the type of audience for which the play was to be performed. It may also signal the growing interest in the masque **genre** in the early part of the seventeenth century.

When studying the play, it is useful to remember the impact that an individual production can achieve. Directors of *The Tempest* have a number of issues to decide relating to their interpretation of the masque in Act IV, Scene 1. It can perhaps only be performed as a magnificent display of Prospero's power but it can be seen as either a father's generous celebration of Miranda's betrothal or an arrogant demonstration of supernatural power from a magician who has managed to win back his power as well as arranging an extremely advantageous marriage for his child. By the use of music, dancing, costume, lighting and position on the stage, a director can influence the audience's perceptions and trigger off a response that will be unique to an individual production.

THE TITLE OF THE PLAY

Storms and tempests have occurred in folk tales throughout recorded history. They were often used to separate natural from supernatural events, and you might like to consider whether, at its most basic level, *The Tempest* is a fairy tale. It certainly involves human beings, spirits and the casting of spells, a handsome prince and a beautiful princess, and the triumph of good over evil.

In more sombre plays such as *Othello* and *King Lear*, Shakespeare uses a storm as a means of cutting the characters off from places and people with whom they were familiar, thus making them re-examine their behaviour and their relationships. *The Tempest* uses a similar

QUESTION

It is often suggested that Shakespeare pays little attention to his choice of titles. How appropriate do you think *The Tempest* is as a title for this play?

technique. It cuts the characters off from the natural world and places them on a mysterious island where love and reconciliation are magically allowed to conquer hatred and envy. The title, therefore, may refer not only to the physical storm that occurs in the first scene of the play, but to the turbulent passions of the characters, passions which, like the storm, are magically transformed into the promise of peace with which the play ends.

The Tempest was almost certainly Shakespeare's last play and it seems probable that it was written in 1611. It was performed in November 1611 at the court of King James and was apparently well received since it was again presented at the court during the winter of 1612–13 when it formed part of the entertainment provided by King James to celebrate the betrothal of his daughter Elizabeth to Frederick, the Elector of the Palatine States, in Germany. *The Tempest* may not have been written specifically for the court, though it does incorporate certain courtly elements, the most obvious of which is the masque in Act IV (see the previous section).

> **CONTEXT**
>
> Although the marriage of Elizabeth and Frederick was not initially of much significance in England, it was ultimately responsible for bringing the Hanoverian line to the British throne in 1714.

In writing his plays Shakespeare frequently made use of existing material, and analogues of *The Tempest* are not hard to find. It would appear, for example, that he knew Montaigne's essay 'Of Cannibals', which was published in English in 1603 and which discussed the value and the way of life of societies which had not been affected by civilisation of a European type.

It seems likely, too, that Shakespeare was affected by the many strange tales being brought back to England by travellers. In particular, he seems to have been influenced by a 1610 pamphlet called *A Discovery of the Bermudas, other wise called the Ile of Divels*. This pamphlet described the adventures of a group of colonists travelling in a convoy of ships from London to Virginia. During the voyage, the flagship was separated from the other ships in a storm and was blown towards Bermuda. The storm tossed the ship onto the rocks but no one on board was drowned. The colonists lived on the island until they had built boats in which they could sail to Virginia. The story of their almost miraculous survival aroused considerable interest in England, and echoes of their adventure can be found in *The Tempest*.

 CHECK THE BOOK

Othello shares several dramatic elements with *The Tempest*. In particular, they both include a character who is not fully conversant with European views and attitudes. Othello is much more sophisticated than Caliban, but he is equally incapable of evaluating the characters of the Europeans with whom he comes into contact.

CHECK THE NET
http://www.idbsu. edu/courses/hy309/ docs/montaigne/ montaigne.04. **html** is a good place to study Montaigne, 'Of Cannibals'.

You might like to question, however, the claim that Shakespeare based his play on the pamphlet or on Montaigne's essay, or on a contemporary German play *Die Schöne Sidea* (*The Lovely Sidea*), which contains similar themes and events. It may seem more likely to you that Shakespeare absorbed traditional and contemporary material and created a play which is not identical in character or treatment with any of his sources.

PART TWO

THE TEXT

NOTE ON THE TEXT

The Tempest was originally printed in the First **Folio** of 1623 and it is remarkably free from inaccuracies and inconsistencies. As well as paying close attention to the language of the play, the Folio editor divides the play into **acts** and scenes and provides detailed stage directions. All subsequent editions of *The Tempest* have been based on the text of the First Folio, although the spelling has been modernised so that words such as 'goe', 'haue' and 'vs', for example, appear as 'go', 'have' and 'us'. The main difference between modern texts is in the numbering of lines. The acts and scenes are the same but the prose text differs in length depending on the size of the font and the width of the page. Since most of the play is, however, written in **blank verse**, the line numbering is not radically different. The text quoted in this book is taken from the current Arden Shakespeare edition (second series), edited by Frank Kermode and published by Methuen & Co. Ltd, London, 1954 (reprinted in 1997 by Thomas Nelson & Sons Ltd).

WWW. CHECK THE NET
For a complete text of the play as it appeared in the 1623 First Folio, see **http://digital.library.upenn.edu/webbin/gutbook/lookup?num=2235**

SYNOPSIS

The play opens with a storm at sea. Alonso, the king of Naples, is sailing home after the marriage of his daughter, Claribel, to the king of Tunis. During the voyage the weather suddenly deteriorates, and Alonso's ship is separated from the rest of the fleet and driven towards an island. The ship hits the coastal rocks and all the passengers leap overboard in the hope of swimming ashore. From this point onward, all the **action** occurs on the island.

In the second scene, we meet Prospero, who had once been the duke of Milan. Prospero explains to his daughter, Miranda, how he had been more interested in books than in safeguarding his position, and so had lost his dukedom twelve years earlier. He had been overthrown by his brother, Antonio, who had received help and

CHECK THE BOOK
The theme of the usurpation of a legitimate ruler occurs frequently in Shakespeare: Claudius takes the throne that should have gone to Hamlet; Macbeth usurps Duncan; and Duke Senior is ousted by his younger brother, Duke Frederick, in *As You Like It*.

support from King Alonso. Antonio and Alonso had ordered an old nobleman, Gonzalo, to abandon Prospero and his young daughter at sea in a leaky boat.

CHECK THE BOOK

In his poem 'Caliban upon Setebos', Robert Browning (1812–89) uses information from the play to meditate on the attributes of God. Caliban approaches God not as a figure from revelation but as a being he believes in from natural reasoning. Caliban has a quick, vivid imagination. He begins with the position of his god in the universe, and then systematically considers Setebos's attributes, and finally attempts to develop rules for worship and service.

Gonzalo, however, had taken pity on them and had provided them with food, drink, clothing and Prospero's beloved books. Prospero and Miranda had been washed ashore on the island and had found one human inhabitant there, a boy of twelve called Caliban. The boy's mother, a witch called Sycorax, had died soon after she had been banished to the island by the ruler of Algiers. At first, Prospero liked Caliban and decided to educate him, but his affection turned to anger when Caliban attempted to rape Miranda. Prospero punished Caliban by enslaving him. Prospero had also found a spirit called Ariel on the island. Ariel had been imprisoned in a tree by Sycorax, but Prospero studied his books and learnt how to set Ariel free by magic. Prospero freed the spirit, but only when Ariel had promised to obey him. Ariel had been obeying one of Prospero's commands when he had caused the storm and apparent shipwreck.

Still under instructions from Prospero, Ariel lures Alonso's son away from the members of his party and leads him towards Prospero's cell. When Ferdinand sees Miranda, he thinks she is a goddess, and Miranda, who has previously only seen her father and Caliban, is equally attracted to the young prince. Prospero is pleased to see that his plan to bring the young people together is working and decides to strengthen their love by putting difficulties in the way of its fulfilment. Accordingly, in spite of Miranda's pleas for mercy, Ferdinand is apprehended as a prisoner and condemned to carry logs.

In the meantime, Alonso believes that his son has been drowned and is filled with grief. Gonzalo tries to console the king but Alonso is irritated by what he regards as false optimism. Their search for Ferdinand has exhausted them and they are forced to lie down and rest. While they are asleep, Antonio, the current duke of Milan, suggests to Sebastian that they could kill Alonso and seize his throne. Ariel, however, has heard their plotting and wakes Gonzalo up in time. Antonio and Sebastian explain that they had drawn their swords to protect the sleeping party from wild animals. Their story is believed and the royal party moves off to continue the search for Ferdinand.

On another part of the island, Caliban meets two of the shipwrecked men: Trinculo, the jester, and Stephano, the butler. Stephano gives him some alcohol and Caliban assumes that he must be a god if he possesses such heavenly liquid. Caliban offers to serve Stephano and make him lord of the island if he agrees to kill Prospero. The three set off to find Prospero, but Ariel becomes aware of the plot, lures them into a stagnant pool where they are trapped up to their necks in mud, and goes to tell Prospero about the plot.

Alonso and his party fail to find Ferdinand but they encounter some spirits who lay out a feast for them. Before they can eat it, however, Ariel disguises himself as a harpy, that is, a mythological character with the body of a woman but the wings and claws of a bird, and reminds them of their sins against Prospero twelve years ago. The feast suddenly disappears and Alonso is overcome by remorse. Antonio and Sebastian, however, are unmoved by Ariel's account of their evil actions.

Prospero watches the manly way that Ferdinand attempts to carry out his punishment and is sufficiently impressed by the young prince's behaviour to agree to his marriage to Miranda. He provides a wedding **masque** to mark their union, but towards the end of it he remembers Caliban's plan to kill him. The three plotters are pursued by spirits who have taken on the shape of large, fierce hounds.

By the last act of the play Prospero has achieved all that he set out to do: he has shown Alonso, Antonio and Sebastian that they had committed a crime against him in banishing him from Milan; they ask for his forgiveness and his dukedom is restored to him. Prospero reveals to Alonso that his son is alive and the friendship between Alonso and Prospero is sealed by the marriage of Ferdinand and Miranda. Prospero frees Ariel and decides to renounce his magical powers. The Boatswain brings news that, in spite of the storm, the ship is seaworthy and ready for the journey to Italy.

> **CONTEXT**
>
> Alonso worries that his sin against Prospero has resulted in the death of his son. The biblical theme of a father's punishment being meted out to his children would have been well known to Shakespeare's audience. The verse 'I the Lord thy God am a jealous God, visiting the iniquity of the fathers upon the children unto the third and fourth generation' occurs in Exodus 20:5 and variants of the verse occur also in Deuteronomy and Numbers.

In the **Epilogue,** Prospero renounces his magic and asks the audience to release him from their spell by the power of their applause.

 CHECK THE BOOK
Read Paul Brown's article in *Political Shakespeare: New Essays in Cultural Materialism*, edited by Dollimore and Sinfield (1994).

There are three points about the conclusion that you might like to think about. The first is Prospero's comment on Caliban: 'this thing of darkness I / Acknowledge mine' (V.1.275–6). It has been suggested by Paul Brown that Prospero is thus acknowledging a link between himself and Caliban. He may be suggesting that his cruelty caused Caliban's bad behaviour, or that there is a core of evil in himself as well as in Caliban.

Secondly, it has been suggested that Prospero's Epilogue is really Shakespeare's farewell to the theatre. It is certainly true that he retired to Stratford soon after the play was written and some of Prospero's words could be interpreted as the playwright's indication of his departure from the stage. Although it would be easy to equate the laying aside of Prospero's magic powers with Shakespeare's relinquishing of his gifts as a dramatist, it would be foolish to force such an interpretation on the play.

Thirdly, John G. Demaray in his book *Shakespeare and the Spectacles of Strangeness: The Tempest and the Transformation of Renaissance Theatrical Forms* (1998) argues that the entire play can be seen as deriving from the masque **genre**. While the betrothal banquet and the scene involving the descent of classical gods are regularly described as masques, other masque elements in *The Tempest* have not been noticed. In particular, some Jacobean masques have a figure called the presenter, who 'releases' performers from the world of the masque and allows them to take their place again in the real world. Such presenters have a role not unlike Prospero's as he releases Alonzo, Antonio and Ariel near the end of the play, and also in the Epilogue as he directly addresses the audience, asking for his own release.

ACT I

SCENE 1

- The action opens on a ship at sea during a wild storm.
- There is noise and confusion everywhere as sailors and passengers struggle to survive.

Most of the **action** of the play takes place on an island. The first scene, however, is a realistic recreation of the dangers of a storm at sea. The ship in distress is carrying Alonso, the king of Naples, from Tunisia, where he and his party had been celebrating his daughter's marriage. The Master of the ship encourages the Boatswain to do all in his power to save the ship but, while he is struggling, he is interrupted by the royal party. The Boatswain knows that they can do nothing to help and so he orders them back to their cabin. Gonzalo tries to comfort the king and his companions by pointing out that the Boatswain has the face of a man who is doomed to be hanged and that, if there is any truth in the proverb 'A man who is born to be hanged will never be drowned', then none of them will perish in the sea. Alonso returns to his cabin but three of the other nobles stay on deck and get in the Boatswain's way. He warns them that their interference may lead to everyone's death. They are not convinced that the Boatswain is fully in control and so they jump overboard in an attempt to swim to the shore.

 CHECK THE NET
You will find excellent material on all aspects of *The Tempest*, including text, performances, productions, theories, paintings and interpretations, by using a search engine such as **www.google.com** and asking for 'Shakespeare The Tempest'.

COMMENTARY

The setting of a storm at sea is a dramatically effective opening. In addition, it provides the audience with a **metaphor** for the past turmoil in the lives of the characters and carries the suggestion, perhaps, that 'after the storm comes the calm'. The opening may remind us of the spectacular storm in *King Lear*, where the king realises how impotent he is. As early as lines 16–17 the Boatswain acknowledges that earthly rulers are powerless against the elemental forces of nature when he asks: 'What cares these roarers for the name of King?'

Shakespeare often uses a storm in his plays as a prelude to a transition from one phase of life to another. We find storms, for example, in *King Lear*, *Macbeth*, *Othello* and *Twelfth Night*, and most members of the audience would have been aware of the significance of tempests in the **Bible** (see **Imagery and symbolism**). The link between tempests and the turbulence of life was regularly employed by writers. In the nineteenth century, the words of the poet Emma Lazarus (1849–87): 'Send these, the homeless, tempest-tossed, to me' were inscribed on the Statue of Liberty as a welcome to immigrants.

The first word we hear in the play is 'Boatswain!', referring to the sailor in charge of the equipment on the ship. The word is pronounced and sometimes written 'bosun'. Although the Boatswain uses 'you', the pronoun of respect, when addressing Gonzalo and the nobles, he is not willing to let them interfere with his efforts to save the ship. He attempts to reduce the surface area of the sail to lessen the wind's pressure and to angle the ship into the wind and so prevent it being driven even closer to the island.

The scene ends with Gonzalo acknowledging that the ultimate control over our lives is not in the hands of human beings. His acceptance of his fate in 'The wills above be done!' (line 66) is reminiscent of the words 'Thy will be done' in the Lord's Prayer.

This first scene is vitally important in catching and holding the attention of an audience. Some of its impact is reduced for a modern audience by changes in language and the loss of proverbs that were well known in Shakespeare's day. In line 7, for example, the Boatswain shouts: 'Blow till thou burst thy wind'. The basic meaning is clear in that he is telling the storm to blow until it blows itself out. In addressing the storm, however, the Boatswain uses 'thou', thus indicating his familiarity with storms and suggesting that all will be well.

In lines 29–30 Gonzalo remarks that the Boatswain's 'complexion is perfect gallows', by which he means that if he judges by the Boatswain's appearance, the man was born to die on the gallows

CHECK THE NET

For a comprehensive film database listing Shakespeare cinematic adaptations, see **http://www.imdb. com/Name? Shakespeare, +William**

rather than to be drowned. Many people in the sixteenth and seventeenth centuries believed that a person's life and death were predestined and that their destiny could not be changed. Gonzalo is suggesting that a person's physiognomy could give insights into their likely death. A similar point is made later when Gonzalo in line 57 urges: 'He'll be hang'd yet', suggesting to Antonio that the Boatswain will be hanged as a criminal even though it looks as if he will drown. The suggestion that the Boatswain's body will be left hanging until it has absorbed so much water that he will burst gives a modern audience a glimpse of the cruelty meted out to criminals at the time. It was usual for a traitor to be 'hanged, drawn and quartered', that is, cut down from the gallows before he had died, then stretched on the rack and finally hacked to death. Noblemen and women were usually treated more leniently: they were beheaded.

In line 42 the Boatswain shows respect for Sebastian's rank by using the 'you' pronoun in 'Work you, then' but no respect for his knowledge of the sea. Basically, he tells Sebastian to save the ship himself or else shut up.

CHECK THE BOOK

A clear example of Shakespeare's awareness of how an 'incorrect' use of 'thou' could be insulting is found in Act III, Scene 2 of *Twelfth Night*. Sir Toby Belch advises Sir Andrew Aguecheek to write to a rival, challenging him to a duel: 'Taunt him with the licence of ink. If thou thou'st him some thrice, it shall not be amiss' (lines 42–4).

GLOSSARY	
3	**yarely** quickly, smartly
16	**roarers** wind and waves; unruly people
40	**pox** venereal disease
48	**unstanched wench** menstruating woman; incontinent young woman
56	**wide-chapp'd** big-mouthed
64	**furlong** one-eighth of a mile, approximately two hundred metres

SCENE 2

- The action in this scene takes place outside Prospero's cell on the island.
- The audience is introduced to the remaining characters and provided with all the background information necessary to understand their actions and motivations.

This very long scene is a means of explaining the background of the play to the audience. It takes place on the island on which the ship has been wrecked. The first inhabitants we meet are Miranda and her father, Prospero. Miranda has seen the shipwreck and asks her father to help the victims, especially if he is responsible for causing the storm. Prospero assures her that no harm has come to anyone and that he has used his magical powers entirely for her sake. Then he tells her their history.

CONTEXT

Milan is the capital of the Lombardy region in Italy. It was an extremely powerful city state in the thirteenth, fourteenth and fifteenth centuries.

Twelve years earlier, when Miranda was not quite three years old, he, Prospero, was the duke of Milan. He had always loved books and had gradually devoted more and more of his time to study, leaving the task of ruling Milan to his brother, Antonio. Slowly but surely, Antonio assumed increased powers until he was in full control of Milan in all but name. In a bid to take over the dukedom completely, Antonio appealed to King Alonso of Naples. He offered to pay Alonso an annual tribute in return for the king's help in dislodging Prospero. Alonso agreed and sent an army to help Antonio to depose Prospero.

CONTEXT

The theme of a younger brother wanting to replace an older brother is found in many folk-tale traditions.

Miranda asks why she and her father were not killed. Prospero tells her that Antonio and Alonso had refrained from killing them because they were afraid of the reaction of the Milanese people, who had always loved him. However, the insurgents condemned Prospero and Miranda to be cast adrift in an old, unseaworthy vessel without sail or oar, in the expectation that they would die at sea. Fortunately, a nobleman called Gonzalo supplied them with food, water, clothing and, most important of all in Prospero's eyes, his beloved books. Because of Gonzalo's help, they had managed to reach their present island, and, as soon as they were established there, Prospero was determined to have the upper hand. At this stage in the narrative, Prospero puts Miranda into a deep sleep so that the spirit Ariel can tell him what has been happening.

Ariel reports that he has obeyed Prospero's commands to the letter. He has separated Alonso's ship from the rest of the fleet, causing them to believe that the king and his party have drowned. He has frightened the courtiers so that they have abandoned ship. He has seen to it that each one of them is safe although their party has been split up. In particular, Alonso's son, Ferdinand, is alone, as Prospero had instructed, the ship is safe in the harbour and the crew is asleep.

Ariel asks Prospero for his freedom and Prospero accuses him of ingratitude. Years before Prospero had arrived on the island, a witch called Sycorax had been banished there from Algeria. While on the island, she had given birth to a son, Caliban, and had imprisoned Ariel in a pine tree. Ariel had been imprisoned in the tree for twelve years, during which time Sycorax had died, and he would have been left in the tree for ever if Prospero had not released him. Ariel is told that he must continue to obey his master or risk being imprisoned in an oak tree. Ariel promises to be obedient and Prospero assures him that, if he does all that is required of him, he will be given his freedom within two days. There are many possible interpretations of Caliban's name. Etymologies have been suggested from Hebrew, Italian and Romani. It is most likely, however, that it is an anagram of 'cannibal', often spelt 'canibal' in the early seventeenth century, or a form of 'Cariban', modern 'Caribbean'.

When Ariel leaves, Prospero wakens Miranda and suggests that they go to see Caliban. Miranda does not like Caliban and does not want to visit him. However, at that moment, he appears carrying firewood for Prospero. Prospero treats Caliban as a slave by day and sends spirits to torment him by night. Caliban curses Prospero and Miranda, claiming that the island had been his until Prospero had used his magic to take it away from him. Caliban insists that Prospero is not only ruthless but hypocritical. When he had first arrived on the island, he had befriended Caliban, teaching him to

CONTEXT

The use and harnessing of magical powers was a subject that exercised the minds of many of Shakespeare's contemporaries. Shakespeare makes use of the theme also in *Macbeth* and *A Midsummer Night's Dream*. One of the best-known figures of the period was a Dr John Dee (1527–1608). He was a superb mathematician but also studied astrology and sorcery. It is likely that he believed his studies of the occult would enable him to call up spirits and control their actions. Dee and his books were so feared that his library was burnt to the ground in the hope that the action would put an end to his unnatural studies.

QUESTION

Do you think that Prospero's character may, in part at least, have been based on Dr Dee?

QUESTION

Examine the suggestion that Prospero controls people by force rather than persuasion.

CHECK THE FILM

Defoe's hero treats Friday a little more humanely than Prospero does Caliban, but he too feels that he has power over a non-European. In *The Life and Adventures of Robinson Crusoe* (made in 1996; released on video in 2000), the storyline was changed to reflect modern attitudes. In it, Crusoe learns to love and respect Friday and the two men discover that they are more likely to survive if they cooperate.

speak. Caliban had, in return, shared his knowledge of the island with Prospero but Prospero had enslaved him. Prospero insists that Caliban had repaid his early kindness by trying to rape Miranda, and Caliban's answer is that he only regrets that the attempted rape had been unsuccessful. Caliban is totally dominated by Prospero.

Ferdinand is lured to Prospero's cave by Ariel's singing. There, he meets Miranda and her father. Ferdinand and Miranda fall in love immediately and Ferdinand, thinking that his father is dead, offers to make her the queen of Naples. Prospero, who had planned the meeting and hoped that the young couple would love each other, decides that Ferdinand must suffer for Miranda. Otherwise he might not value her highly enough. Accordingly, he uses his magical powers to imprison Ferdinand, and Ferdinand feels that his imprisonment will be worthwhile if it enables him to see Miranda. Miranda is upset with her father but feels certain that Ferdinand's imprisonment will not last long.

COMMENTARY

Islands have often been selected by writers as a means of allowing characters to develop in isolation. Such a setting was employed by Daniel Defoe for *Robinson Crusoe* (1719) and, more recently, by William Golding in *Lord of the Flies* (1954). In both *The Tempest* and *Lord of the Flies*, the island may be seen as a microcosm of the world at large. Shakespeare also uses the theme of one brother being usurped by another in *As You Like It*. In this play, the senior brother lives with some followers in the forest of Arden but also regains his dukedom.

Although this play deals with the exercise of magical powers, it also includes many biblical references that would have been more immediately significant in the seventeenth century, For example, in line 30 Prospero assures Miranda that not even a hair of anyone's head will be lost. This would have reminded an Elizabethan audience of St Luke's Gospel 12:7, where Jesus tells his followers that God loves them so much that 'the very hairs of your head are all numbered'.

This is one of the longest and most significant scenes in the play. It introduces us to the main characters and provides the necessary background information. It indicates Miranda's sensitivity to the plight of others. In her first speech, she tells her father: 'Had I been any god of power, I would / Have sunk the sea within the earth' (lines 10–11), suggesting that she would have caused the earth to swallow up the sea rather than allow the ship to sink with all its passengers and crew still on board. The fact that she appeals to her father to do what she cannot is the first indication we have of Prospero's magical powers. This suggestion is strengthened in line 25, when Prospero addresses his gown: 'Lie there, my Art'. The gown is a **symbol** of his magic powers. Sorcerers' gowns were often richly adorned with symbols of the occult. In line 77 he admits that he was 'rapt in secret studies' and the use of both 'rapt' and 'secret' suggests that he was studying magic. This suggestion is reinforced by the use of 'transported' in the previous line. To be 'transported' could mean 'conveyed out of one's body to another place'.

Line 61 introduces a theme that recurs in Shakespeare's plays. Miranda asks if it was perhaps a good thing that they were exiled: 'Or bless'd was't we did?' In several of his plays, a deposed ruler sometimes finds a kind of happiness in his exile. King Lear learns the value of truth and loyalty when he has given up his throne, and Duke Senior finds the forest of Arden preferable to the superficiality of courtly life in *As You Like It*. Prospero and Duke Senior may comment on the providential nature of their exile, but neither hesitates for a moment to take over his dukedom when it becomes available.

In examining Prospero's character, we should be careful not to rely too heavily on his self-evalution. In the speech beginning on line 89, he tells Miranda that he neglected the affairs of state in order to devote himself to his studies; that he trusted his brother completely and gave him absolute power; that the power brought out the faults in Antonio's character; and that Antonio's evil was in sharp contrast to Prospero's generosity. Perhaps we should remember that being a ruler involves both rights and responsibilities. Prospero wanted the former but not the latter.

There are three other themes in this scene that should be stressed because of their relevance to the play. The first is astrology, which

> **CONTEXT**
> 'Wench' did not necessarily have a pejorative meaning in Shakespeare. It could be used as an endearment (as in line 139) by a father to a daughter.

ties in with Prospero's study of the occult but which was also a perfectly legitimate area of learning. In line 182 Prospero refers to the 'most auspicious star' that led them to the island. This is a reference to the widely held belief that our lives and fortunes are influenced by the movements of the stars and planets. The second theme is the interest in the new discoveries. In line 229, for example, Ariel refers to 'the still-vex'd Bermoothes', meaning 'the perpetually stormy Bermudas'. The islands were named after the Spanish seaman, Juan de Bermudez, who mapped them early in the sixteenth century. Even in Shakespeare's day there were stories in circulation about the sudden fierce storms in the area that came to be known as the Bermuda Triangle.

The third point to stress is the language used in connection with Caliban. His mother is referred to as 'The foul witch Sycorax' (line 258). It should be remembered that witches were feared in Shakespeare's day and could be put to death. It is suggested in line 269 that Sycorax would, in fact, have been killed except for the fact that she was pregnant. Although the usual penalty for being a witch in Shakespeare's day was death by hanging or burning, the death penalty was not carried out if the woman was pregnant. The reference to her being 'blue-ey'd' would have meant something very different to Shakespeare's audience. Blue-tinged eyelids were traditionally thought to be an early sign of pregnancy. The use of 'litter' to mean 'give birth to' in line 282 reduces Caliban to the level of an animal. Notice how often animal terminology is applied to Caliban, for example 'whelp' in line 283 and 'dam' in line 322. This was one method used by Prospero to stress Caliban's supposed inferiority. In line 321 Prospero goes further and suggests that Caliban was 'got by the devil', meaning 'fathered by an evil spirit'. This is not the straightforward insult that it might appear to a modern audience. In Shakespeare's day it was believed that a woman could have intercourse with an incubus or male demon, and this was regarded as a sin for which there was no forgiveness.

In spite of Prospero's debasing of Caliban, the 'salvage and deformed' slave's reference to the sun and the moon in line 337 as 'the bigger light' and 'the less' would have reminded his audience of the language of the newly translated King James Bible (1611).

CHECK THE BOOK

The theme of intercourse with a spirit occurs also in *Doctor Faustus*, a play written by Christopher Marlowe (1564–93) probably in 1588. When Faustus conjures up Helen of Troy, his audience would have believed her to be a succubus, or female devil, capable of having intercourse with Faustus. You might like to compare the characters of Faustus and Prospero. Before he dies, Faustus too is willing to give up his books, but by then it is too late for him. There are other similarities between Prospero and Faustus. Just as Faustus controls Mephastophilis for a certain period, so too does Prospero control Ariel.

In Genesis I:16 we are told: 'And God made two great lights; the greater light to rule the day, and the lesser light to rule the night'.

GLOSSARY		
1	**Art** magical powers	
4	**welkin** sky	
13	**fraughting souls** human cargo	
14	**amazement** consternation, horror	
20	**poor cell** poor man's dwelling	
28	**provision** foresight	
35	**bootless inquisition** useless questioning	
56	**piece of virtue** very essence of virtue	
59	**no worse issued** equally nobly born	
64	**teen** trouble, pain, grief	
71	**signories** dukedoms, states	
73	**liberal Arts** theoretical knowledge	
125	**presently** immediately	
180	**prescience** foresight, planning	
207	**coil** tumult, uproar	
384	**burthen** chorus or refrain of a song, usually spelt 'burden'	

CONTEXT

Setebos was the name given to a Patagonian god. He is first mentioned in the travel accounts of Ferdinand Magellan (1480–1521). Magellan was a Portuguese explorer who left Spain in 1519 to sail around the world. He spent time in South America and recorded his experiences with Amerindians.

ACT II

SCENE 1

- The action moves to another part of the island.
- The audience learns more about the shipwrecked passengers and about Antonio's lack of remorse for his crime against Prospero.
- Ariel prevents the murder of Alonso.

The new **act** takes us to the part of the island where Alonso and his party have been washed ashore. Alonso is depressed because he believes that his son, Ferdinand, has been drowned. He finds little consolation in Gonzalo's suggestions that Ferdinand may still be alive and that their own survival is something to be grateful for. Far from sympathising with his brother's apparent loss, Sebastian rubs salt in the wound by suggesting by the phrase 'sweet marriage' (line 69), which could mean 'profitable marriage', that Claribel's marriage may have been undertaken for economic rather than romantic reasons. If this suggestion is true, then Alonso might feel that his treatment of a daughter has been punished by the loss of a son. Later, in lines 119–21, Sebastian makes his criticism overt by telling Alonso that he 'may thank [himself] for this great loss' because he has not allowed his daughter to marry a European prince but has given her to an African. His expression in line 121 that he has 'loose[d] her to an African' is unfeeling and also racist. There is just the suggestion here, too, of the **plot** of *Othello*, where Desdemona, the Venetian, marries Othello, the Moor or North African.

Gonzalo philosophises on the ideal state, a type of 'commonwealth' where labour and rewards are equally shared by all members of the community. Alonso finds the old man's comments tiresome, but Antonio and Sebastian mock Gonzalo both for his views and for the dull way he expresses them.

Ariel, who is invisible to the castaways, casts a spell on them to make them drowsy. They all fall asleep except for Antonio and Sebastian. Seeing how unprotected Alonso is, Antonio urges Sebastian to seize his chance, kill Alonso and take his brother's throne for himself, in the same way that he, Antonio, had usurped Prospero and become the duke of Milan.

Sebastian succumbs to Antonio's temptation. He offers to kill Gonzalo if Antonio kills Alonso, and he promises Antonio that the tribute he currently pays to Naples will be cancelled once Alonso is dead. Before they can carry out the murders, however, Ariel sings in Gonzalo's ear, waking him up. Gonzalo rouses the king, who demands to know why Sebastian and Antonio have their swords out. Sebastian and Antonio pretend that they had drawn their swords to protect their sleeping companions from wild animals. Their explanation is accepted and the group sets out in search of Ferdinand.

CONTEXT

Dido was the queen of Carthage at the time of the Trojan War. In Virgil's *Aeneid*, Dido fell in love with the shipwrecked Aeneas, the founder of Rome. They got married, but although he was happy, he left her to fulfil his destiny. Dido committed suicide when she realised that Aeneas had betrayed her. The linking of the marriage of Alonso's daughter with Dido raises questions in the minds of the audience, suggesting that Claribel's initial happiness may be a prelude to pain and desertion.

COMMENTARY

One of the themes of the play is relationships: between brothers (Antonio and Prospero, Alonso and Sebastian); between fathers and children (Prospero and Miranda, Alonso and Ferdinand); between 'masters' and 'slaves' (Prospero and Ariel, Prospero and Caliban); between men and women (Caliban and Miranda, Ferdinand and Miranda). The characters of Sebastian and Antonio are developed here. They are both witty and skilful at wordplay but they are also both seemingly unaffected by the suffering of others. Sebastian's comment that Alonso 'receives comfort like cold porridge' in line 10 is ambiguous. He may mean that the comfort being provided by Gonzalo is valueless or that Alonso is not in the mood to be comforted. Either way, he and Antonio show little sympathy for the sufferings of others. They joke with each other throughout the scene. Although Prospero ultimately forgives Antonio and Sebastian for their treachery, there is no evidence that either man truly repents.

This is one of the many scenes in which Shakespeare draws references from classical mythology. The juxtaposition of Claribel and Dido allows him to suggest that Claribel's fate may not be a happy one but also to remind the audience of the Golden Age, which leads on to Gonzalo's thoughts on the ideal state. In classical mythology there was a belief in an early 'golden' age when people lived in justice and harmony and when there was abundant food, no wars and work was optional. This period shares similarities with the biblical description of the Garden of Eden.

GLOSSARY		
34	desert uninhabited land	
41	delicate exquisite; sexually experienced	
42	temperance mild climate	
88	kernels pips	
136	chirurgeonly surgeon-like	
139	plantation colonisation	
146	Letters education, learning	
159	foison abundant harvest	continued

CONTEXT

Shakespeare's audience would probably have had a better grounding in classical mythology than a modern audience. Within a few lines there are references to Dido and Aeneas, to the site of ancient Carthage and to the Greek legend that the walls of Thebes rose when Amphion played his harp.

CONTEXT

When Gonzalo refers to 'the moon out of her sphere' (line 178), he is alluding to the system of astronomy described by Ptolemy. According to the Ptolemaic system, the moon, sun and stars circled the earth, each in its own fixed sphere. The reference to 'flat' in line 176 might also be seen as a reinforcement of the once commonly held view that the earth was flat.

252	**cubit** approximately fifty centimetres
268	**feater** more gracefully
269	**fellows** equals

QUESTION

Examine Scene 2 closely, paying particular attention to Caliban's complaints against Prospero, and evaluate how these criticisms affect your response to the characters of both Caliban and Prospero.

SCENE 2

- The action moves to another part of the island.
- This scene provides details about the original island dwellers. It was intended to provide comic relief and is sometimes described as an antimasque because it parallels the **masque** in its use of music, movement and unusual costumes.

In this scene the audience is encouraged to focus on Caliban. Caliban is cursing Prospero, who makes him carry firewood by day and sends spirits to torment him by night. When he sees Alonso's court jester, Trinculo, he thinks that he must be one of Prospero's spirits and decides to hide in the hope that he will avoid more pain. Trinculo has swum ashore and is looking for somewhere to hide from the rain. When he sees Caliban's cloak, he thinks it is some strange outcrop on the island and crawls under it for shelter.

Alonso's butler, Stephano, comes along and sees a cloak on the ground with four legs sticking out of it. Stephano had reached the island by clinging to a barrel of wine and it is clear that he has already had a lot to drink. He questions the 'thing' on the ground and is amazed when he gets an answer. After some knockabout farce, Trinculo and Caliban reveal themselves and Stephano shares his wine with them. It is Caliban's first taste of alcohol and he believes that the man who can provide such heavenly liquid must be a god. He offers to serve Stephano in the hope that Stephano will free him from Prospero's yoke. The three move off drunkenly so that Caliban can show them the treasures of his island.

COMMENTARY

This scene encourages the audience to think about colonisation. It also expresses the view that some groups of people are less able to control the effects of alcohol. Such a view was held about many of the colonised people, including the Native Americans. Shakespeare often gives the audience a clue to character in the **imagery** used. Much of Trinculo's imagery is related to drinking, whereas Caliban's is more tuned to nature and to the ruling of his island.

In thinking about this subject, we must be careful to avoid **anachronisms**. We know a great deal about the evils of slavery and the problems associated with colonisation. When Shakespeare wrote this play, however, British colonisation was in its infancy, with settlers in Ireland and North and South America only. In addition, few writers of the day questioned the rights of Europeans to colonise other countries.

Prospero has enslaved Caliban in the way that many colonising countries enslaved the people of the countries they 'discovered'. The Nigerian writer Chinua Achebe writes about Europeans who claimed to have 'discovered' Nigeria in the fifteenth century, pointing out that, for the local people, Nigeria had never been lost.

This comic scene presents a number of difficulties for a modern director and audience. The first difficulty is in its kind of slapstick comedy. It relies on **punning**, which is no longer found so amusing, on a knowledge of proverbs that are not current and on an attitude to physical differences that is politically incorrect. The punning relates mainly to drinking and sexual behaviour. For example, Stephano refers to '*itch*' in his song (line 54). The song refers to sexual desires but also probably to the effects of sexually transmitted diseases. It is certainly true that scabies, a skin infection and not a sexually transmitted disease, was also sometimes called 'the itch', but there can be little doubt that Stephano is singing about sexual desire and its gratification. There is further punning in the equating of having a drink with kissing the **Bible** in line 121. The suggestion is that the bottle is, like the Bible, an object to swear on. At the time, it was not unusual to kiss the Bible to confirm that everything one had said was the truth.

 CHECK THE NET

Trinculo's comments on making money by showing Caliban off in a sideshow are grotesque from a modern point of view, but information on such 'freak shows' can be found at **http://www.nyam.org/library/historical/teratology/popular.shtml**

 CHECK THE NET

For an essay on colonialism and *The Tempest*, see **http://www.about-shakespeare.com/**

Two examples of proverbial usage can be found in lines 84–5 and 99–100. In the former, Stephano says: 'here is that which will give language to you, cat'. This is a reference to the proverb: 'Ale can make a cat talk'. In lines 99–100 he continues: 'This is a devil, and no monster: I will leave him; I have no long spoon.' This is a reference to another proverb: 'He should have a long spoon that sups with the devil', which means that it is imperative to think before taking action.

Thirdly, there is the treatment of Caliban as someone to be exploited. He is described as a 'moon-calf' in line 107. A Shakespearean audience would have understood this to imply that Caliban was deformed. Deformities in human beings and animals were often explained by suggesting that they were conceived when the moon was full. We no longer share this view but it is still widely believed that the moon has an effect on our behaviour. Earlier in the scene, in lines 28–34, Trinculo suggests that if he were in England and had even a painting of this fish-like 'creature', he would display it outside a booth at a fair and everyone would pay to go inside and stare at the monster. The references here and in the following lines give some indication of the treatment of people of other cultures. They were often taken to Europe and treated like exotic animals for people to pay and stare at. The phenomenon of the freak show did not die out until the early twentieth century. People paid to see animals such as three-legged chickens as well as human beings who were either excessively tall or short or fat or thin. In Shakespeare's day Native Americans were occasionally displayed at fairs to the curious. Often the Indians did not survive long and so the dead bodies were 'exhibited'.

There is, perhaps, a hidden clue to Prospero's magical powers in this scene. In lines 81–2 Caliban tells Trinculo: 'Thou dost me yet but little hurt; thou wilt anon, I know it by thy trembling'. Trembling was often regarded as a prelude to demonic possession. The fact that Caliban recognises this may indicate that Prospero sometimes behaves like a man possessed.

CHECK THE FILM

Prospero's Books is a free adaptation of the play, starring John Gielgud as Prospero (1991, directed by Peter Greenaway). The change in title indicates the different emphasis.

GLOSSARY

3	**inch-meal** little by little, inch by inch
9	**mow** make faces, grimace
21	**bombard** a large leather container for holding liquids, often alcohol
32	**doit** coin of very little value. Members of Shakespeare's audience would have understood the reference here. It is to beggars on the streets. Elizabeth I (d.1603) had issued proclamations to encourage the repatriation of both Irish and 'Blackamoor' beggars
39	**gaberdine** rough cloak, outer garment. You might like to consider the use of garments as a means of marking out one type of character from another on the Shakespearean stage. Another character who wears a gaberdine is Shylock in *The Merchant of Venice*
51	**tang** sting. Stephano puns on *'tongue'* and *'tang'* since the words were probably homophones in his day
61	**proper** handsome, fine
71–2	**neat's-leather** cowhide, cow's leather
107	**vent** excrete
143	**anon** immediately
147	**sooth** truth
168	**pig-nuts** possibly groundnuts, truffles or edible tubers
171	**filberts** hazelnuts
172	**scamels** seabirds

ACT III

SCENE 1

- The first scene in this **act** takes place near Prospero's dwelling.
- Miranda and Ferdinand express their love for each other.

Unknown to the young couple, Prospero watches while Miranda tries to help Ferdinand in his 'slavery'. She offers to carry some of the logs for him, but Ferdinand assures her that his hard work gives

CONTEXT

Prospero's behaviour in watching the young couple might look like voyeurism, but few people of Shakespeare's day would have questioned his right to look after his daughter's interests.

him pleasure because he is toiling for her. Ferdinand confesses that he has fallen under the spell of other beautiful women in the past but always found some weakness in them. He now believes, however, that he has found perfection in Miranda.

They confess their love for each other and promise to get married as soon as it is possible. Prospero is delighted that his plan is working and that such deep affection has developed between his daughter and the son of the king of Naples.

COMMENTARY

Modern readers may react strongly against Prospero's punishment of Ferdinand. It is worth stressing that, for the purposes of dramatic **unity** (see **Dramatic unities**), however, Prospero has to show that the young couple's love is deep and abiding, rather than the result of physical attraction. Romantic love was a frequent theme in the Shakespearean theatre. It was less common in life, especially among the wealthy, where marriages were often arranged like other transactions that increased or guaranteed prosperity.

There are three textual points that should be clarified. In the very first lines, Ferdinand assures Miranda:

> There be some sports are painful, and their labour
> Delight in them sets off …

By this he means that some types of suffering are worthwhile because they eventually bring great joy and delight. His reasoning here is not unlike Prospero's, who has suggested that if Miranda is too easily won, she will not be sufficiently appreciated.

Later, in line 70, Miranda asks Ferdinand frankly if he loves her, and he replies that he hopes to miss out on any of the good fortune that lies ahead of him, if he lies about the sincerity of his feelings. The open acknowledgement of their love leads to the third point to require a comment. Between lines 87–9 Miranda uses the word 'husband' and Ferdinand gives her his 'hand'. The meaning of this section is often lost on contemporary audiences, but in Shakespeare's day these words could have constituted a marriage.

CHECK THE BOOK

Shakespeare makes a similar suggestion in Act I, Scene 2 of *Henry IV, Part 1,* where Prince Hal suggests that we only truly appreciate something if it is unusual and also if we have invested a considerable amount of effort to attain it.

Weddings were usually performed in church in front of witnesses, but neither of these was necessary for the marriage to be valid.

GLOSSARY		
2	baseness	humiliation
6	quickens	brings to life
8	crabbed	annoying, bad-tempered
11	sore injunction	an order that will result in severe punishment if it is not obeyed
31	infected	madly in love
32	visitation	visit
37	hest	command
43	several	individual
53	skilless	ignorant
63	flesh-fly	a fly known to carry germs
	blow	soil, lay eggs in
84	maid	both 'servant' and 'virgin'
	fellow	companion, equal

CHECK THE FILM

A 1968 film of *The Tempest*, directed by Basil Coleman, starred Ronald Pickup as Ariel.

SCENE 2

- The action shifts to another part of the island.
- This humorous scene concentrates on Caliban, Stephano and Trinculo, and provides interesting insights into the treatment of 'difference' in the seventeenth century.

In this scene we meet Caliban, Stephano and Trinculo again. Ariel also takes part in the **action** but he is invisible to the other three. Caliban has been telling Stephano about Prospero and Miranda and encouraging him to kill Prospero and take over control of the island. Trinculo does not like Caliban, and Ariel contributes to the dislike by imitating Trinculo's voice and calling Caliban a liar. Stephano tells Trinculo to leave Caliban alone, but Ariel calls him a liar too. Stephano assumes that Trinculo is the culprit and hits him.

Trinculo attributes the strange behaviour of Stephano and Caliban to the alcohol they have drunk.

Stephano encourages Caliban to tell them more about Prospero. Caliban reveals that Prospero is helpless without his books and that if Stephano steals them, he will be able to kill Prospero while he is having his afternoon nap. Stephano decides to kill Prospero and take over Miranda and the island. Trinculo decides to accompany Stephano and Caliban, and Ariel rushes off to tell Prospero about the conspiracy.

COMMENTARY

The attitude to Caliban expressed by Stephano and Trinculo is, by today's standards, politically incorrect and totally unacceptable. It is worth remembering, however, that circuses and sideshows exhibiting so-called 'freaks' were popular even in the twentieth century. Caliban may be foolish in thinking that Stephano and Trinculo are worthy of his service, but he never loses sight of the fact that the island is his and that Prospero 'hath cheated me of the island' (lines 41–2).

One of the linguistic devices used by Shakespeare to create comedy is **punning**. Sometimes the puns are sexual but in this scene they are simply a device to entertain the audience. Stephano begins the double entendres in line 8, where the meaning of 'set' is 'set in a fixed stare', and is continued by Trinculo in lines 9–10, where 'set' means 'placed'. The joking continues in lines 15–16, where 'standard' is used to mean 'flag carrier' and then 'able to stand without support'.

 CHECK THE BOOK

Today, punning is rarely as highly prized as it was in Shakespeare's day. A full introduction to the complexity of Shakespearean puns can be found in Frankie Rubinstein's *A Dictionary of Shakespeare's Sexual Puns and Their Significance* (1995).

GLOSSARY	
4	**folly** absurdity
13	**five-and-thirty leagues** about one hundred miles
16	**list** want, wish, please
38	**Marry** an oath, originally 'By the Blessed Virgin Mary'
50	**Mum** silence
62	**pied ninny** multicoloured fool
	patch jester

66	**quick freshes** springs of fresh water
78	**murrain** plague
89	**wezand** windpipe
91	**sot** fool, idiot
98	**nonpareil** unequalled for beauty
115	**troll the catch** sing the song in parts, loudly and with gusto
116	**while-ere** a little while ago, not long ago
119	***Flout*** mock
	cout make a fool of
120	***scout*** sneer at

SCENE 3

- This scene moves to another part of the island.
- It involves a miming masque and provides Alonso with the opportunity to express his remorse for his behaviour towards Prospero.

 QUESTION

Examine the use of the **masque** in this scene as a mechanism for allowing Alonso to express remorse for his treatment of Prospero.

This scene opens with the royal party, and the audience discovers that Antonio and Sebastian are still determined to kill Alonso. They plan to do it in the evening, when people are tired and less vigilant. When the group decides to rest, Prospero appears with some spirits and they spread a feast out in front of the hungry men. When they try to eat it, however, Ariel appears in the guise of a harpy and reminds them of their cruelty to Prospero and Miranda. Ariel and the feast then disappear. Alonso is filled with grief for the crime he committed against Prospero, but Antonio and Sebastian are unmoved and decide to fight the spirits of the island.

COMMENTARY

The introduction of a feast that is spread before them but which they cannot eat is reminiscent of earlier **morality plays**.

CHECK THE BOOK

The description of strange beings in other lands is reminiscent of the claims made by Othello in I.3.144–5 when he tells Desdemona of his encounters with 'The Anthropophagi, and men whose heads / Do grow beneath their shoulders'.

CONTEXT

Raleigh spent years planning a voyage to Guiana. He probably believed that the discovery and conquest of an Incan empire would bring him personal glory and wealth, as well as raising his profile at court. In 1595 he therefore went in search of El Dorado. The expedition was a failure but his account of it, *Discoverie of Guiana*, is still a fascinating work.

Shakespeare is eclectic in his use of material drawn from different periods and cultures. In this scene, there are references derived from Christianity. They occur in line 1: 'By 'r lakin', meaning 'By Our Little Lady', which is a reference to the Blessed Virgin Mary; in line 20, where 'keepers' implies 'guardian angels'; and in line 53, where Alonso, Antonio and Sebastian are called 'three men of sin'. There is also an assumption that the audience will be familiar with classical mythology. In line 22 we hear about unicorns, the legendary horses with one horn in the centre of their foreheads. This is immediately followed in line 23 with a mention of the phoenix, the fabled bird that built its own funeral pyre and burnt to death, only to regenerate itself by rising from the ashes. There is also an appearance of a harpy in line 53. This is a monster with the face of a woman but the wings and talons of a vulture. A third type of information that can be gleaned from the scene relates to voyages of discovery and the stories carried back to Europe by travellers. In line 48 we encounter the phrase 'Each putter-out of five for one', meaning 'each traveller'. In Shakespeare's day it was common practice for men to deposit a sum of money before going on a long journey. If they did not return or if they did not complete the journey, they forfeited their deposit. If they were successful, however, they got five times the amount of the original sum. The description of the strange beings found in foreign lands in lines 44–7 is similar to one appearing in the 1596 account in Walter Raleigh's writings on Guiana, South America, of a 'nation of people whose heads appear not above their shoulders … they are reported to have their eyes in their shoulders, and their mouths in the middle of their breasts'.

Modern audiences tend to miss topical references such as that in lines 2–3 to the 'maze' with its 'forth-rights and meanders'. The Hampton Court maze with its winding paths and problem routes was constructed in 1608 and was regarded as a gardening achievement worthy of being visited by newcomers to London.

GLOSSARY

10	frustrate useless, futile
12	repulse setback
21	drollery puppet show

30	**certes** certainly
39	**dumb discourse** mime
61	**elements** materials, constituents
65	**dowle** small feather
79	**wraths** ghosts; anger
83	**Bravely** excellently
101	**plummet** a plumb line, a line with a weight on the end of it causing it to sink
108	**ecstasy** madness

ACT IV

SCENE 1

- Now the action moves to the front of Prospero's dwelling.
- This long scene includes a masque to celebrate the love of the young couple.
- Caliban's plot to murder Prospero is prevented.

Prospero decides that Ferdinand has suffered enough and so he agrees to let him marry Miranda. To celebrate their betrothal he organises a **masque,** which is performed by spirits under the direction of Ariel.

The spirits take the forms of Greek and Roman goddesses. First Iris, the Greek goddess of the rainbow and the messenger of the gods, appears. She introduces Juno, the Roman queen of the gods, and then Ceres, the Roman goddess of fertility and of the harvest. Their speech is poetic and emphasises the joys of marriage. Ferdinand is delighted with the spectacle, but there is more to come. Iris calls up the naiads, or spirits of the waters, and they are followed by a group of reapers. The naiads and reapers dance together and their disappearance brings the masque to an end.

CONTEXT

Roman gods:
Jupiter, king of the gods
Juno, queen of the gods
Venus, goddess of love
Cupid, son of Venus
Ceres, goddess of the harvest
Neptune, god of the sea
Dis, god of the underworld

Greek gods:
Iris, goddess of the rainbow
Hymen, god of marriage
Phoebus, god of the sun

The sudden termination of the festivities is caused by Prospero's remembering that Caliban, Stephano and Trinculo are planning to kill him. He apologises to Ferdinand and leaves the young lovers so that he can deal with the three conspirators.

Ariel is called and explains that he has led the three plotters into a stagnant, muddy pool. Ariel is told to bring out some of Prospero's rich garments and hang them on the trees to distract Stephano and Trinculo. Prospero and Ariel then make themselves invisible so that they can watch what happens.

Trinculo, Stephano and Caliban arrive. The first two are annoyed with Caliban because they have lost their wine in the pool. They see the clothes that have been hung up by Ariel and quarrel about who should keep them. Caliban tries to tell them that the garments are merely trash and that their sole concern should be the murder of Prospero. Trinculo and Stephano refuse to listen to Caliban, however, and while they are preparing to carry off the clothes, Prospero and Ariel call up spirits in the shape of hounds, which chase the three away from Prospero's cell.

QUESTION

There are elements of potential tragedy in *The Tempest*. Examine these and show how the audience is made aware that these elements will not be allowed to prevail.

COMMENTARY

The potential for tragedy that has hung over this play since the first scene is gradually abating. Love triumphs and 'treachery' is discovered. In theory, Caliban was guilty of insurrection, but Shakespeare emphasises that Caliban has always regarded the island as his and that he was less motivated by greed than the more 'civilised' Trinculo and Stephano.

In this scene Shakespeare makes use of characters from Greek and Roman mythology. Hymen is often regarded as the Greek god of marriage and his appearance signals that the union between Miranda and Ferdinand is being blessed in heaven as well as on earth. Phoebus is the god of the sun, and day lasts as long as his chariot takes to drive round the heavens. Ferdinand longs for night to come and thinks that the horses of the sun god must be lame since the day is so long! Iris is the goddess of the rainbow and also a messenger from the gods. The rainbow is also the Old Testament **symbol** of a pact between God and humanity. Ceres is the harvest or corn goddess and her appearance signals fruitfulness and fertility. Venus is the goddess of love and Cupid her blind son. He often caused havoc by making people fall in love with inappropriate partners, but his arrows have found their appropriate marks with Miranda and Ferdinand. Dis is the ruler of the underworld, and so this group suggests that heaven, the earth and the underworld are united in this celebration.

CHECK THE BOOK

The Oxford Dictionary of Phrase and Fable (edited by Elizabeth Knowles, Oxford University Press, 2000) is an extremely useful reference book for information on many of the allusions in the play.

GLOSSARY

7	**strangely**	wonderfully, extremely well
16	**sanctimonious**	holy, sacred
18	**aspersion**	sprinkling with holy water, blessing
24	**issue**	children
37	**rabble**	group, band of people or spirits
41	**vanity**	illusion, manifestation of power
42	**Presently**	immediately
43	**with a twink**	very rapidly
47	**mop and mow**	grimaces, with appropriate facial expressions
60	*leas*	arable land
63	*stover*	hay
64	*pioned*	dug
	twilled	woven
	brims	edges
81	*bosky*	wooded
110	*foison*	rich, abundant harvest
156	**rack**	small cloud

ACT V

SCENE 1

- The last scene is again played in front of Prospero's dwelling.
- The play ends with hope for the future, with forgiveness for earlier wrong, with freedom for Ariel, and with Caliban again in control of his island.

Prospero's plans are now reaching fulfilment, so he sends Ariel to bring the royal party to his cell. Alonso, Sebastian and Antonio have been kept in a distracted state by one of Prospero's spells. Prospero reveals himself to the party, rebukes Alonso, Antonio and Sebastian for the evil they have done, then forgives them all and thanks Gonzalo for his kindness. Alonso still believes that his son is dead but Prospero shows him the young couple playing chess. Alonso rejoices in their happiness and adds his blessing to their proposed marriage.

Ariel next brings in the ship's captain and the Boatswain and they tell the company that the ship is seaworthy and ready for the journey back to Italy.

Finally, Ariel leads in Trinculo, Stephano and Caliban. The jester and the butler are reprimanded by Alonso. Caliban admits that he was foolish to regard Stephano as a god and he promises: 'I'll be wise hereafter, / And seek for grace' (lines 294–5).

Prospero agrees to resume his dukedom in Milan but first he invites the royal party to spend the night in his cell and listen to the story of the last twelve years. In keeping with his promise, he releases Ariel.

COMMENTARY

When Prospero renounces his magic in lines 54–7, he is perhaps acknowledging the limitations of his power:

> ... I'll break my staff,
> Bury it certain fadoms in the earth,

CHECK THE BOOK

Compare Prospero's renunciation of magic in V.1.33–57 with Medea's incantations in Ovid's *Metamorphoses*, VII.179–219.

And deeper than did ever plummet sound
I'll drown my book.

He could control the elements but not change the hearts of Antonio
or Sebastian; he could punish Caliban but not make him abandon
his claim to the island or give up his worship of his own god,
Setebos.

By the end of Act V all the **sub-plots** are integrated; tragedy has
been averted; love and reconciliation are stressed. The audience
might subsequently wonder why Antonio and Sebastian are treated
so much more leniently than Caliban was, but the play ends on a
note of hope.

GLOSSARY		
36	demi-puppets	small, doll-like fairies
316	chick	dear one

EPILOGUE

- Prospero addresses the audience.

Prospero assures his listeners that he has laid aside his magical
powers, has forgiven his enemies and has been given back his
dukedom. All he needs now is to be set free from the spell cast
on him by the audience, and this can be done by their applause.

COMMENTARY

The **Epilogue** gains depth if we believe that it is not only a fitting
conclusion to *The Tempest* but is also Shakespeare's valediction to
the theatre. It is true that this was probably the last play completely
written by Shakespeare and it is also true that many of Prospero's
words could apply to the playwright. However, it is probably best
to be sceptical about the equation. The Epilogue is a fitting
conclusion to a play that deals with the supernatural and that is
more **masque**-oriented than any of his other plays. It is always risky

 QUESTION

Do you think
that Prospero's
Epilogue is
an essential
component of
The Tempest?
(Ask yourself if
it is a satisfactory
denouement
or an artistic
appendage.)

? QUESTION

The Tempest
involves a three-
plot structure of
betrayal, love and
forgiveness. How
are these plots
developed and
reconciled?

to identify writers too closely with their creations. Of course
they tap into their own experiences in their creative works, but
it would be as foolish to identify Shakespeare with Prospero as it
would to regard Emma as a biographical clue to the character of
Jane Austen. However, it does no harm to compare Shakespeare's
skill as a great playwright to Prospero's skill as an accomplished
magician.

EXTENDED COMMENTARIES

Four passages have been selected from *The Tempest* to illustrate
different aspects of the text, for example dialogue and monologue,
verse and prose, and to examine some themes and techniques (see
Critical approaches).

TEXT 1 – I.1.1–67

> [*On a ship at sea*]: *a tempestuous noise of*
> *thunder and lightning heard.*
> *Enter a Ship-Master and a Boatswain.*

MASTER: Boatswain!

BOATSWAIN: Here, master: what cheer?

MASTER: Good: speak to th' mariners: fall to 't, yarely, or
we run ourselves aground: bestir, bestir.   *Exit.*

> *Enter Mariners.*

BOATSWAIN: Heigh, my hearts! cheerly, cheerly, my hearts!   5
yare, yare! Take in the topsail. Tend to th' master's
whistle. Blow till thou burst thy wind, if room
enough!

> *Enter* ALONSO, SEBASTIAN, ANTONIO, FERDINAND,
> GONZALO, *and others.*

ALONSO: Good boatswain, have care. Where's the master?
Play the men.   10

BOATSWAIN: I pray now, keep below.

ANTONIO: Where is the master, boatswain?

BOATSWAIN: Do you not hear him? You mar our labour: keep
    your cabins: you do assist the storm.

GONZALO: Nay, good, be patient.   15

BOATSWAIN: When the sea is. Hence! What cares these roarers
    for the name of the King? To cabin: silence! trouble
    us not.

GONZALO: Good, yet remember whom thou hast aboard.

BOATSWAIN: None that I more love than myself. You are a   20
    counsellor; if you can command these elements to
    silence, and work the peace of the presence, we will
    not hand a rope more; use your authority: if you
    cannot, give thanks you have lived so long, and
    make yourself ready in your cabin for the mischance   25
    of the hour, if it so hap. Cheerly, good hearts! Out
    of our way, I say.   *Exit.*

GONZALO: I have great comfort from this fellow: methinks he
    hath no drowning mark upon him; his complexion
    is perfect gallows. Stand fast, good Fate, to his   30
    hanging: make the rope of his destiny our cable, for
    our own doth little advantage. If he be not born
    to be hanged, our case is miserable.   *Exeunt.*

    Re-enter Boatswain.

BOATSWAIN: Down with the topmast! yare! lower, lower!
    Bring her to try with main-course. *A cry within.* A   35
    plague upon this howling! they are louder than the
    weather or our office.

    [*Re-*]*enter* SEBASTIAN, ANTONIO, *and* GONZALO.

    Yet again! what do you here? Shall we give o'er,
    and drown? Have you a mind to sink?

SEBASTIAN: A pox o' your throat, you bawling, blasphemous,   40
    incharitable dog!

BOATSWAIN: Work you, then.

ANTONIO: Hang, cur! hang, you whoreson, insolent noise-
    maker. We are less afraid to be drowned than thou
    art.   45

**www. CHECK
THE NET**
See **http://the-tech.
mit.edu/
Shakespeare/
tempest** for the
complete play; this
is useful if you wish
to search for an
elusive word or
quotation.

GONZALO: I'll warrant him for drowning, though the ship
were no stronger than a nutshell, and as leaky as an
unstanched wench.

BOATSWAIN: Lay her a-hold, a-hold! set her two courses; off to
sea again; lay her off.   50

Enter Mariners wet.

MARINERS: All lost, to prayers, to prayers! all lost!

BOATSWAIN: What, must our mouths be cold?

GONZALO: The King and Prince at prayers, let's assist them,
For our case is as theirs.

SEBASTIAN: I'm out of patience.

ANTONIO: We are merely cheated of our lives by drunkards: 55
This wide-chapp'd rascal, – would thou mightst lie drowning
The washing of ten tides!

GONZALO: He'll be hang'd yet,
Though every drop of water swear against it,
And gape at wid'st to glut him.
  A confined noise within: "Mercy on us!" –
"We split, we split!" – "Farewell, my wife and children!" –   60
"Farewell, brother!" – "We split, we split, we split!"

ANTONIO: Let's all sink wi' th' King.

SEBASTIAN: Let's take leave of him.
                              Exeunt [ANTONIO *and* SEBASTIAN].

GONZALO: Now would I give a thousand furlongs of sea for an
acre of barren ground, long heath, broom, furze,   65
anything. The wills above be done! but I would fain
die a dry death.   *Exeunt.*

CONTEXT

In line 57 Antonio uses the phrase 'the washing of ten tides'. It was customary in Shakespeare's day for the bodies of pirates to be left hanging on the shore until three tides had come in and gone out. This punishment was meant to be a warning to others of the dangers of piracy. Antonio thinks the Boatswain is such a criminal that his body should be exposed to ten tides.

This passage comes from the beginning of the play and is meant to capture and hold the attention of the audience, to introduce some of the characters and themes, and to suggest the nature of the drama about to unfold.

In spite of the confusion caused by danger, this passage allows us to make a number of deductions about the characters introduced. Some of them are designated by their trade, for example 'Boatswain' and 'Master', whereas others have first names, such as Alonso and Gonzalo. An obvious inference from this is that the audience will get to know the latter group. These are characters whose story is about to unfold. The courtly characters are, perhaps, so used to being obeyed that they attempt to interfere in the Master's attempts to ride the storm. Even within this broad generalisation, however, we can detect three distinct attitudes. Alonso is worried but courteous ('Good boatswain, have care', line 9); Antonio and Sebastian are inconsiderate and rude ('A pox o' your throat', line 40, and 'whoreson, insolent noise-maker', lines 43–4), and they put their own safety before that of the king (line 63); and Gonzalo attempts to be a peacemaker (line 15), is talkative (lines 28–33), good-humoured (lines 46–8), attentive to Alonso's needs (line 53) and willing to accept his fate with courage (lines 66–7).

Since these are the first words an audience hears, we would expect certain interests and recurrent themes to be established. These include the significance of the storm; the potential feud between Alonso and his brother; the willingness of Alonso to repent (he is, after all, 'at prayers' in line 53); the suggested closeness between Alonso and the prince, in that they are travelling together; and Gonzalo's loyalty to the king.

Even in this short scene, there are indications of the quick passage of time. There are six entrances and five exits, suggesting a great deal of activity over a period of time, and the Boatswain gives instructions that must take time to carry out. There is also time for the king to attempt to find out what is happening and then go below to pray; and Antonio and Sebastian can decide not to drown with the king but to save themselves.

The language is relatively easy to understand in context, although some of the vocabulary and many of the structures are no longer current. A modern audience would have to guess the meaning of such words as 'yarely', 'bestir', 'cheerly' and 'roarers', but might notice that such words are more likely to occur in the speech of the mariners. A modern audience might also notice the use of 'do' where it seems unnecessary, as in 'you do assist the storm' (line 14), and its non-use in forming questions: 'What cares these roarers ...?'

 CHECK THE NET
See **http://www. online-literature. com/shakespeare/ tempest/** for a comprehensive scene-by-scene summary of the play, together with readers' comments and reviews.

(line 16). Speed is indicated in the use of orders rather than statements and in the reduction of structures, for example: 'if room enough' (if there is room enough) and 'have care' (have a care) (lines 7–9). An attentive observer might notice that Gonzalo uses 'thou' to the Boatswain but receives 'you' back (lines 19–26), thus stressing the difference in rank. Alonso's style of address is courteous; the mariners are unwilling to tolerate interference even from people of much higher rank.

The most significant images and **symbols** here are of struggle and suffering: the strength and noise of the storm (e.g. line 7, line 36 and line 47); death by drowning (line 29); death by hanging (line 30); and barrenness (line 65).

TEXT 2 – I.2.285–346

PROSPERO: Dull thing, I say so; he, that Caliban,   285
    Whom now I keep in service. Thou best know'st
    What torment I did find thee in; thy groans
    Did make wolves howl, and penetrate the breasts
    Of ever-angry bears: it was a torment
    To lay upon the damn'd, which Sycorax   290
    Could not again undo: it was mine Art,
    When I arriv'd and heard thee, that made gape
    The pine, and let thee out.

ARIEL: I thank thee, master.

PROSPERO: If thou more murmur'st, I will rend an oak,
    And peg thee in his knotty entrails, till   295
    Thou hast howl'd away twelve winters.

ARIEL: Pardon, master:
    I will be correspondent to command,
    And do my spriting gently.

PROSPERO: Do so; and after two days
    I will discharge thee.

ARIEL: That's my noble master!
    What shall I do? say what; what shall I do?   300

PROSPERO: Go make thyself like a nymph o' th' sea:
    Be subject to

CHECK THE BOOK

Percy Bysshe Shelley (1792–1822) wrote a poem in 1822 about Ariel and Miranda called 'With a Guitar, to Jane'; the opening lines begin 'Ariel to Miranda'.

> No sight but thine and mine; invisible
> To every eyeball else. Go take this shape,
> And hither come in 't: go: hence   305
> With diligence.   *Exit* [ARIEL].
> Awake, dear heart, awake! thou hast slept well;
> Awake!

MIRANDA: The strangeness of your story put
Heaviness in me.

PROSPERO: Shake it off. Come on;
We'll visit Caliban my slave, who never   310
Yields us kind answer.

MIRANDA: 'Tis a villain, sir,
I do not love to look on.

PROSPERO: But, as 'tis,
We cannot miss him: he does make our fire,
Fetch in our wood, and serves in offices
That profit us. What, ho! slave! Caliban!   315
Thou earth, thou! speak.

CALIBAN *within*:   There's wood enough within.

PROSPERO: Come forth, I say! there's other business for thee;
Come, thou tortoise! when?

> [*Re-*]*enter* ARIEL *like a water-nymph.*

Fine apparition! My quaint Ariel,
Hark in thine ear.

ARIEL: My lord, it shall be done.   *Exit.* 320

PROSPERO: Thou poisonous slave, got by the devil himself
Upon thy wicked dam, come forth!

> *Enter* CALIBAN.

CALIBAN: As wicked dew as e'er my mother brush'd
With raven's feather from unwholesome fen
Drop on you both! a south-west blow on ye   325
And blister you all o'er!

PROSPERO: For this, be sure, to-night thou shalt have cramps,
Side-stitches that shall pen thy breath up; urchins
Shall, for that vast of night that they may work,
All exercise on thee; thou shalt be pinch'd   330

**CHECK
THE FILM**
Derek Jarman
directed a 1980
version of *The
Tempest,* starring
Heathcote Williams
as Prospero and
Toyah Willcox as
Miranda. See
**http://us.imdb.
com/Title?0081613**
for a complete cast
list and a review of
the film.

CHECK THE FILM

A 1982 film of the play, starring Susan Sarandon and directed by Paul Mazursky, has an architect leaving his unfaithful wife to live on a Greek island with his daughter. There is only one other person on the island, a goatherd with severe learning difficulties.

> As thick as honeycomb, each pinch more stinging
> Than bees that made 'em.
>
> CALIBAN: I must eat my dinner.
> This island's mine, by Sycorax my mother,
> Which thou tak'st from me. When thou cam'st first,
> Thou strok'st me, and made much of me; wouldst give me   335
> Water with berries in 't; and teach me how
> To name the bigger light, and how the less,
> That burn by day and night: and then I lov'd thee,
> And show'd thee all the qualities o' th' isle,
> The fresh springs, brine-pits, barren place and fertile: 340
> Curs'd be I that did so! All the charms
> Of Sycorax, toads, beetles, bats, light on you!
> For I am all the subjects that you have,
> Which first was mine own King: and here you sty me
> In this hard rock, whiles you do keep from me   345
> The rest o' th' island.

This passage comes from the second scene of the first **act** and is significant in introducing the audience to the island dwellers. Prospero's power is stressed and perhaps the audience is encouraged to think of Prospero as a godlike figure, whose power one admires but whose actions are not always understood. We are also invited to compare and contrast Prospero's attitude to Ariel and to Caliban.

The characters reveal themselves in what they say and how they say it, what they do and how they do it, and in their behaviour towards others. Prospero's first words – 'Dull thing' – reduce Caliban from a person to an inanimate object. He controls Ariel more by a technique known as 'carrot and stick' (line 299 offers freedom and line 295 the pain of being imprisoned). Prospero's attitude to Miranda is much kinder ('dear heart', line 307), but she is kept totally in the dark about Ariel, who must remain invisible to everyone but Prospero (lines 302–4). Prospero needs Caliban's work (lines 313–15) but treats him as a 'slave' (line 315), as lazy and slow (line 318), and insults his mother, whom he suggests mated with the devil (lines 321–2). Miranda clearly states her dislike of Caliban (lines 311–12), but her use of 'it' in line 311: ''Tis a villain' should not be misunderstood. In Shakespeare's day 'it' was frequently used where we would use 'he' (see **Language and style**).

Caliban may be enslaved but his speech is anything but servile. He is prepared to suffer excruciating cramps (lines 323–7) rather than accept the insult to his mother. His belief in his right to the island is one of the first things we hear him say (line 333). Whereas Ariel is prepared to do everything that Prospero wants as a means of gaining eventual freedom, Caliban insists that he should not have to earn his freedom because the island, and all that it produces, is his.

These four characters are among the most important in the play and Shakespeare associates them with the major recurring themes. Prospero is associated with magic ('mine Art', line 291) and power, often cruel (lines 295 and 327); Miranda with innocence (lines 308–9 show that Miranda has no idea that her father used his powers to make her sleep). Ariel is associated with beauty (line 301), speed (line 319) and enjoyment of work (line 320); and in Caliban we can see the themes of courage and strength of character (lines 323–6), love of the island (lines 333–46) and the attitude towards coloniser (lines 333–46).

Although this part of Scene 2 can be acted in five minutes, we are given an impression of time passing by a number of references. The distant past when Sycorax was alive and Ariel trapped in a tree (lines 286–7) is conjured up, as is a glimpse of the future when Ariel will be free (lines 298–9), and the more recent past when Prospero arrived and treated Caliban well (line 335). We are also informed of the regularity with which Caliban performs his menial tasks (lines 313–15), the fact that Miranda has been asleep (line 307), and that Ariel can transform himself into a nymph (line 301).

The language and style in this scene vary subtly to imply different attitudes, characters and topics. Ariel and Caliban both use 'thou' to Prospero, Ariel's use suggesting intimacy, Caliban's an unwillingness to accept his enslavement. Miranda uses 'you' to her father, stressing her respect. Prospero is used to being obeyed and uses more commands than any other character (lines 301–5 and 317–18). He also uses 'I' more than the others, again suggesting his

> **CONTEXT**
>
> In his plays, Shakespeare shows understanding of people who have suffered because they were in some way 'different'. This is especially true of Caliban in *The Tempest* and Shylock in *The Merchant of Venice*. Is it possible that his father's loss of money and prestige due to his adherence to the religion of his childhood taught Shakespeare sensitivity to people who did not conform?

power and self-absorption, especially since the 'I' frequently occurs with verbs of doing, punishing and rewarding.

Miranda says very little here but shows respect for her father. She is much less critical of Caliban, saying only that he is a villain and that she does not like to see him (lines 311–12). Ariel uses address terms such as 'master' (line 296) and 'lord' (line 320), suggesting that he is willing to appear servile if it wins his freedom. Caliban, on the other hand, does not use one courteous term of address; he is prepared to suffer for the sake of cursing both Prospero and Miranda (lines 323–6). Caliban uses verse throughout, suggesting that, in spite of being enslaved, his spirit is free and he is keenly aware of natural beauty (lines 336–46).

The **imagery** in this section is associated with pain and suffering (threatened for Ariel and Caliban by Prospero and in Caliban's curse), beauty (line 301) and animal imagery, for example wolves, beasts, bears, tortoise, raven, bees, toads, beetles and bats. These are, with the exception of the first three, associated with Caliban. Only the first three are dangerous mammals, whereas the others might be seen as lower-order animals, suggesting Prospero's attitude to Caliban's position in the natural hierarchy.

CONTEXT

Miranda and Ferdinand fall in love the moment they see each other. A Shakespearean audience would have accepted this convention and been reminded of a couplet from Christopher Marlowe's poem *Hero and Leander* (published 1598): 'Where both deliberate, the love is slight; / Who ever loved that loved not at first sight?'

TEXT 3 – III.1.15–74

> *Enter* MIRANDA; *and* PROSPERO [*at a distance, unseen*].

MIRANDA: Alas now, pray you,   15
   Work not so hard: I would the lightning had
   Burnt up those logs that you are enjoin'd to pile!
   Pray, set it down, and rest you: when this burns,
   'Twill weep for having wearied you. My father
   Is hard at study; pray, now, rest yourself: 20
   He's safe for these three hours.

FERDINAND: O most dear mistress,
   The sun will set before I shall discharge
   What I must strive to do.

MIRANDA: If you'll sit down,
   I'll bear your logs the while: pray give me that;
   I'll carry it to the pile.

FERDINAND: No, precious creature;   25
   I had rather crack my sinews, break my back,
   Than you should such dishonour undergo,
   While I sit lazy by.

MIRANDA: It would become me
   As well as it does you: and I should do it
   With much more ease; for my good will is to it,   30
   And yours it is against.

PROSPERO: Poor worm, thou art infected!
   This visitation shows it.

MIRANDA: You look wearily.

FERDINAND: No, noble mistress: 'tis fresh morning with me
   When you are by at night. I do beseech you, –
   Chiefly that I might set it in my prayers, –   35
   What is your name?

MIRANDA: Miranda. – O my father,
   I have broke your hest to say so!

FERDINAND: Admir'd Miranda!
   Indeed the top of admiration! worth
   What's dearest to the world! Full many a lady
   I have ey'd with best regard, and many a time   40
   Th' harmony of their tongues hath into bondage
   Brought my too diligent ear: for several virtues
   Have I lik'd several women; never any
   With so full soul, but some defect in her
   Did quarrel with the noblest grace she ow'd,   45
   And put it to the foil: but you, O you,
   So perfect and so peerless, are created
   Of every creature's best!

MIRANDA: I do not know
   One of my sex; no woman's face remember,
   Save, from my glass, mine own; nor have I seen   50
   More that I may call men than you, good friend,
   And my dear father: how features are abroad,
   I am skilless of; but, by my modesty,
   The jewel in my dower, I would not wish
   Any companion in the world but you;   55

CHECK THE BOOK

W. H. Auden's lengthy, semi-dramatised poem 'The Sea and the Mirror' (1944) is subtitled 'A Commentary on Shakespeare's *The Tempest*'.

> Nor can imagination form a shape,
> Besides yourself, to like of. But I prattle
> Something too wildly, and my father's precepts
> I therein do forget.
>
> FERDINAND: I am, in my condition,
> A prince, Miranda; I do think, a King;   60
> I would not so! – and would no more endure
> This wooden slavery than to suffer
> The flesh-fly blow my mouth. Hear my soul speak:
> The very instant that I saw you, did
> My heart fly to your service; there resides,   65
> To make me slave to it; and for your sake
> Am I this patient log-man.
>
> MIRANDA: Do you love me?
>
> FERDINAND: O heaven, O earth, bear witness to this sound,
> And crown what I profess with kind event,
> If I speak true! if hollowly, invert   70
> What best is boded me to mischief! I,
> Beyond all limit of what else i' th' world,
> Do love, prize, honour you.
>
> MIRANDA: I am a fool
> To weep at what I am glad of.

CHECK THE BOOK

You might like to compare the declaration of love between Ferdinand and Miranda with that expressed by the young couple Florizel and Perdita in *The Winter's Tale*.

This third passage is a dialogue between the two young lovers. Ferdinand has been forced to carry logs so that Prospero can test the depth of his regard for Miranda and prevent him thinking that Miranda is too easily won. Prospero, unseen, watches the two and is moved by their gentle consideration of each other.

Only the audience is aware that there are three characters in this scene, and it is possible to regard Prospero either as a peeping Tom or as a father who wants only the best for his innocent daughter. (You might like to compare the scene in Milton's *Paradise Lost* where Satan enters the Garden of Eden and watches Adam and Eve before the fall. He is so struck by their beauty and innocence that, in Milton's words, he sat 'stupidly good'.)

Miranda is generous and considerate, willing to share Ferdinand's punishment. He is equally determined that he will not allow her to suffer on his behalf. There is no artifice in Miranda. She responds to Ferdinand's compliments by saying that she loves him and would like to be his wife (lines 54–5 and 83–6). Indeed, she is the one who moves their relationship along by asking: 'Do you love me?' (line 67). Ferdinand stresses his love by saying that, although he is a prince, he is glad to labour for her sake (lines 59–67).

Love, in its many forms, is thematic in *The Tempest*. This scene reveals the falling in love and the development of love between Miranda and Ferdinand, shown in their kindness to each other and their willingness to suffer for each other; as well as the love of a father for a daughter; and the interrelationship between love and power: Prospero plans the love in order to win back his dukedom; Ferdinand is willing to forgo his princedom if it means he can have Miranda.

Time is of little significance to the lovers, but it is indicated by Ferdinand's references to other women he has known (lines 39–42); Miranda's stressing her ignorance of men; and Prospero's reference to the fact that Miranda has been 'infected' (line 31).

The interchanges between Miranda and Ferdinand are among the most poetic in the play. They use 'you' to each other, stressing their mutual respect but also emphasising the fact that they have not known each other long. Their dialogue is a series of questions and answers where they provide each other and the audience with information about the past and with a clear indication of the beauty of their characters.

Apart from Prospero's reference to Miranda as a 'Poor worm' (line 31) there is no animal **imagery** here. Instead, we find references to pain (line 16); natural phenomena: lightning (line 16), fresh morning (line 33), night (line 34); music (line 41); body parts: eyes, tongues, ears (lines 40–2); and jewels (line 54).

CHECK THE BOOK

Ted Hughes wrote a poem to his late wife, Sylvia Plath, called 'Setebos', which was published in his *Birthday Letters* (1998). It begins: 'Who could play Miranda? / Only you. Ferdinand – only me.'

TEXT 4 – V.1.290–318 AND EPILOGUE, LINES 1–20

PROSPERO: He is as disproportion'd in his manners   290
   As in his shape. Go, sirrah, to my cell;
   Take with you your companions; as you look
   To have my pardon, trim it handsomely.

CALIBAN: Ay, that I will; and I'll be wise hereafter,
   And seek for grace. What a thrice-double ass   295
   Was I, to take this drunkard for a god,
   And worship this dull fool!

PROSPERO: Go to; away!

ALONSO: Hence, and bestow your luggage where you found it.

SEBASTIAN: Or stole it, rather.

PROSPERO: Sir, I invite your Highness and your train   300
   To my poor cell, where you shall take your rest
   For this one night; which, part of it, I'll waste
   With such discourse as, I not doubt, shall make it
   Go quick away: the story of my life,
   And the particular accidents gone by   305
   Since I came to this isle: and in the morn
   I'll bring you to your ship, and so to Naples,
   Where I have hope to see the nuptial
   Of these our dear-belov'd solemnized;
   And thence retire me to my Milan, where   310
   Every third thought shall be my grave.

ALONSO: I long
   To hear the story of your life, which must
   Take the ear strangely.

PROSPERO: I'll deliver all;
   And promise you calm seas, auspicious gales,
   And sail so expeditious, that shall catch   315
   Your royal fleet far off. [*Aside to* ARIEL.] My Ariel, chick,
   That is thy charge: then to the elements
   Be free, and fare thou well! Please you, draw near.

                        Exeunt omnes.

? QUESTION

How relevant to a study of *The Tempest* is a knowledge of the theatre for which Shakespeare wrote?

Epilogue

Spoken by PROSPERO.

> *Now my charms are all o'erthrown,*
> *And what strength I have's mine own,*
> *Which is most faint: now, 'tis true,*
> *I must be here confin'd by you,*
> *Or sent to Naples. Let me not,*   5
> *Since I have my dukedom got,*
> *And pardon'd the deceiver, dwell*
> *In this bare island by your spell;*
> *But release me from my bands*
> *With the help of your good hands:*   10
> *Gentle breath of yours my sails*
> *Must fill, or else my project fails,*
> *Which was to please. Now I want*
> *Spirits to enforce, Art to enchant;*
> *And my ending is despair,*   15
> *Unless I be reliev'd by prayer,*
> *Which pierces so, that it assaults*
> *Mercy itself, and frees all faults.*
>   *As you from crimes would pardon'd be,*
>   *Let your indulgence set me free.*   Exit.   20

This passage comes from the end of the play and brings to a conclusion not only the action but the imaginary world that has been created. Prospero assigns the future of the island to Caliban and Ariel, says what his own plans are, and addresses the audience directly as he breaks through the boundaries of fact and fantasy.

Three of the main characters, among others, are present at the end of the play, namely Prospero, Caliban and Ariel. As on many occasions in the play, Prospero is in control and directs their actions and their destinies. Caliban is shown as apparently seeing the error of his ways. Although Prospero criticises his behaviour, Caliban knows that his freedom is imminent, and he accepts his fate without question. Ariel takes his last order from Prospero. He will ensure good weather for the ships, and then receive his freedom.

 CHECK THE BOOK

It is not uncommon for a seventeenth-century play to end with an **epilogue**. You might like to compare Prospero's Epilogue with Rosalind's in *As You Like It,* a play that shares a central idea with *The Tempest* in the exile of a duke due to the usurpation of his dukedom by a younger brother.

Prospero seems to have everything in control. He gives orders to
Caliban and Ariel, and in a more respectful way directs Alonso to
his cell. In the Epilogue, Prospero exerts the ultimate control by
ending the illusion that has been created, returning the scene from
the island to the wooden stage.

**www. CHECK
THE NET**
http://www.
sparknotes.com/
shakespeare/
tempest/ is a useful
site with sections on
themes, character
analysis and
context. Always
read such material
with a degree of
detachment.

Power is one of the constant themes in *The Tempest*. Prospero is
giving up his magical powers and his total control of Caliban and
Ariel, but he is still directing events. He is reclaiming his dukedom,
but he is relinquishing the powers that allowed him to hold sway
on the island ('*my charms are all o'erthrown*', Epilogue, line 1).
Ultimately, Prospero is given the power to bring the play to an end.
Since the **masque** is also a **motif** in *The Tempest*, Prospero is bringing
to a resolution the structural and thematic elements of the drama.

Prospero pardons his brother for taking his dukedom (Epilogue,
line 7), but should it be Prospero himself who should be seeking
forgiveness for having neglected his people and his responsibilities?
Forgiveness is mentioned again at the end of the play, when
Prospero calls upon the audience to release him. The value of good
judgement is repeated here. Caliban says: 'I'll be wise hereafter'
(line 294), and Prospero assures Alonso that on his return to Milan:
'Every third thought shall be my grave' (line 311). In other words,
he will prepare himself for his death and eternity.

CONTEXT

The link between
'cannibal' and
'Caribbean' is
closer than we
might guess. The
English word
comes from
Spanish *canibal*,
which was used by
Christopher
Columbus as a
variant form of
Caribes, the name
applied to some of
the indigenous
people of Cuba
and Haiti.

Freedom and duty, linked throughout the play, are balanced at the
end. In exchange for his final task, Caliban will gain his freedom
(lines 291–3). So, too, will Ariel, once he has given the fleet fair
weather (lines 316–18). Prospero will take on the duties of his
dukedom and give up the liberty of his magical powers, leaving
himself at the mercy of the audience: '*I must be here confin'd by
you, / Or sent to Naples*' (Epilogue, lines 4–5).

This extract marks the transition from the timescale of the play to
that of the real world, and the contrast highlights how unreal the
world of the island has been. During Act V the actions and words
belong within the realm of the illusion, but the Epilogue brings
the audience back to the real world. The transition is marked by
Caliban's 'I will' and 'I'll be wise hereafter' (line 294) which refer

to a future that we will not witness. Prospero's words to Alonso summarise the events of the whole play in two lines: 'the particular accidents gone by / Since I came to this isle' (lines 305–6). Then he moves on to the immediate future: 'and in the morn / I'll bring you to your ship, and so to Naples' (lines 306–7).

At the start of the Epilogue there is a time reference – '*Now*' – that marks the transition from the realm of the imagination to the theatre in which the play has taken place. Both time and location have been transformed.

The language echoes many of the ideas that have been explored already in *The Tempest*. The issue of acceptable and unacceptable appearance and behaviour is raised again (lines 290–1), and the interest in magic and charms is repeated (lines 317–18 and Epilogue, lines 8 and 14). The end of Act V is in keeping with much of the play in consisting of conversation between the characters. The lines are in verse in the form of iambic **pentameters**. In the Epilogue, however, there is a marked change. The poetry is in rhyming couplets, each line having four stressed syllables. The change in style would impress on the audience the fact that some significant dramatic change is taking place.

The references here combine the familiar animal **imagery** associated with Caliban (line 295) and a type of deliberate ambiguity in the Epilogue. Prospero refers to a '*bare island*' (line 8) which could be the island of the play. However, it is linked with '*this*' and '*your spell*', where the 'you' he is addressing directly is the audience. Prospero's reference to '*your good hands*' (line 10) and '*Gentle breath of yours my sails*' (line 11) refers back to the ships but also signifies a request for applause. His use of words like '*Spirits to enforce, Art to enchant*' (line 14) reminds us of the magical realm of the island, but now they are superseded by a more Christian prayer as the two final lines echo the Lord's Prayer: 'Forgive us our sins as we forgive those who sin against us.'

The **Extended commentaries** above are not meant to be exhaustive. They show only how the themes and techniques described in **Critical approaches** are useful tools in the response to, and description of, texts.

> **CONTEXT**
>
> Shakespeare uses rhyming couplets in most of his plays. These are sequences of the same length and pattern, in which each two lines rhyme. Rhyming couplets are particularly useful for expressing ideas succinctly, as when they are used to conclude a sonnet: 'But if thou live remembered not to be, / Die single, and thine image dies with thee' (Sonnet 3). The witches open *Macbeth* using rhyming couplets: 'When shall we three meet again? / In thunder, lightning, or in rain? / When the hurlyburly's done, / When the battle's lost and won.'

PART THREE

CRITICAL APPROACHES

CHARACTER EVALUATION

Critics in different countries and at different times have offered varying evaluations of the characters in *The Tempest*. For some, Prospero is an almost godlike figure appearing magnanimous for forgiving his brother and Alonso, for freeing Ariel, and for treating Caliban well until he attempted to rape Miranda. Others, especially critics from colonised countries, describe Prospero as an oppressive invader who seeks to dominate both Caliban and Ariel. It was probably not Shakespeare's intention to alienate his audience from either the coloniser or the colonised. In his day there was a widely held belief that our place in society was divinely ordained and that a country got the ruler it deserved. Read the play carefully. Evaluate what is said and make up your own mind.

Shakespeare's characters are usually subtly drawn. Like living human beings, they are rarely completely good or completely bad, and can show different sides of their nature depending on the people they are with or the circumstances in which they find themselves. In *The Tempest*, however, it has been suggested that the main characters are at one and the same time naturalistic and representational. At one level, the four main characters on the island may be said to represent different attributes of humanity: instinct – Caliban; love – Miranda; spirit – Ariel; and power – Prospero.

But such a generalisation should be challenged and discussed rather than simply accepted. It does, however, seem true that in his last plays, *Pericles*, *The Winter's Tale* and *The Tempest*, Shakespeare is more interested in dealing with human weaknesses and human destiny than in delineating highly idiosyncratic characters.

It has often been suggested that, with the exception of Miranda, all of the characters in *The Tempest* undergo a transformation as soon as they reach the island. Like many generalisations, this one needs to be examined carefully. We might ask if Prospero himself

CHECK THE BOOK

After reading Shakespeare's *The Tempest*, you might like to compare it with Aimé Césaire's reworking of it as *A Tempest* (*Une tempête, d'après La tempête de Shakespeare: adaptation pour un théâtre nègre*, 1969). Césaire's is a **symbolic** work about white domination of blacks.

experiences any change of heart. He certainly tells the audience that he has decided to treat the transgressors with mercy rather than with the revenge that he had earlier planned, and, before the final **act**, he voluntarily relinquishes his magical powers in order to take up his birthright, the dukedom of Milan. Alonso certainly changes. He feels remorse for his sin against Prospero and feels that he has been punished for it in the apparent loss of his son. Ferdinand changes in the sense that he falls in love and recognises that this love is more real than any he has previously experienced. It is highly debatable if the others change. Antonio, Sebastian, Trinculo and Stephano all succumb to temptation and are all forgiven, but it is unlikely that they have experienced any change of character.

PROSPERO

Prospero plays the most significant role in the play in that he is on the stage longer than any other character and he controls the fate of all the others on the island. You might like to consider whether he uses his powers wisely and humanely or selfishly. His name means 'fortunate' or 'prosperous' and you might like to examine how fortunate he is in the kindness he received from Gonzalo and in his ability to win back his dukedom.

He lost his dukedom because he failed to recognise his brother's ambition and because he neglected his first duty, the governing of Milan. As he himself tells Miranda:

> The government I cast upon my brother,
> And to my state grew stranger, being transported
> And rapt in secret studies. (I.2.75–7)

His treatment by his brother, Antonio, has taught him not to trust appearances. It may look as if Ferdinand loves Miranda, but Prospero is determined to test the strength of this love:

> They are both in either's pow'rs: but this swift business
> I must uneasy make, lest too light winning
> Make the prize light. (I.2.453–5)

You might ask yourself if Prospero is as affectionate and caring as he suggests. For example, he tells Miranda that: 'I have done

CHECK THE NET

Shakespeare often uses Italian settings and personal names in his plays, possibly because Italy was so closely linked to the Renaissance and gave a sense of the exotic to his drama. A good source of background on his knowledge and use of Italian culture can be found at **http://shakespeare authorship.com/ italy.html**

nothing but in care of thee, / Of thee, my dear one; thee, my daughter' (I.2.16–17), although it was his behaviour that caused Miranda's fate in the first place. His attitude towards others should also be considered. He seems to love Ariel: 'Do you love me, master?' asks the spirit. 'Dearly, my delicate Ariel' (IV.1.48–9), yet he can behave cruelly to him:

CONTEXT

Find out about the life of Christopher Marlowe (1564–93) and assess his possible influence on his contemporary, Shakespeare. Is the Prospero figure influenced by Marlowe's dabbling in the occult? Is Shakespeare influenced by *Doctor Faustus*?

> ... malignant thing! Hast thou forgot
> The foul witch Sycorax, who with age and envy
> Was grown into a hoop? has thou forgot her? (I.2.257–9)

Prospero also shows love for, and gratitude towards, Gonzalo, describing him as 'A noble Neapolitan, Gonzalo' (I.2.161); and later, when he meets Gonzalo face to face, he is moved to tears by the old man's goodness: 'Holy Gonzalo, honourable man, / Mine eyes, ev'n sociable to the show of thine, / Fall fellowly drops' (V.1.62–4).

Prospero remembers the evil of Alonso, Antonio and Sebastian but forgives them:

> Though with their high wrongs I am struck to th' quick,
> Yet with my nobler reason 'gainst my fury
> Do I take part: the rarer action is
> In virtue than in vengeance: they being penitent,
> The sole drift of my purpose doth extend
> Not a frown further. (V.1.25–30)

His harshness towards Caliban must rate as Prospero's greatest weakness. It is true that Caliban tried to rape Miranda: 'thou didst seek to violate / The honour of my child' (I.2.349–50), but the language he uses to Caliban seems unnecessarily severe: 'Thou most lying slave, / Whom stripes may move, not kindness! I have us'd thee, / Filth as thou art, with human care' (I.2.346–8), and it is vindictive to plague Caliban, who is only twenty-four, with arthritis:

> Hag-seed, hence!
> Fetch us in fuel; and be quick, thou 'rt best,
> To answer other business. Shrug'st thou, malice?

> If thou neglect'st, or dost unwillingly
> What I command, I'll rack thee with old cramps,
> Fill all thy bones with aches, make thee roar,
> That beasts shall tremble at thy din. (I.2.367–73)

It is an interesting psychological truth that it is easier to hurt people if we debase them in our own minds. One of the simplest ways of doing this is to use language to diminish the person. If Prospero describes Caliban using non-human **metaphors** such as 'hag-seed' or 'litter', it is a short step to treating him as subhuman.

Prospero is the central character and must sustain the interest of the audience. He can be played as a powerful and magnanimous man or as a cruel sorcerer. There is evidence of both possibilities in the play.

CALIBAN

Caliban is, to a modern audience, one of the most interesting and sympathetic characters in the play. He is described in the **Folio** edition of *The Tempest* as 'a salvage and deformed slave'. The word 'salvage' is an earlier form of modern 'savage', but in Shakespeare's day it meant 'wild and uncivilised' rather than 'cruel' or 'bestial'. Most people in England believed that uncivilised people were below their civilised counterparts in the hierarchy that had God at its apex and inanimate nature at its base. However, some were beginning to question this assumption, and there is evidence in the play that Shakespeare believed that the corruption in so-called 'civilised' society was more abhorrent than any natural behaviour.

Caliban's name may be an anagram of 'cannibal', often spelt with one 'n' in Shakespeare's day, or it may derive from 'Cariban' since people in England were familiar with stories about Carib Indians. Caliban's deformity is never exactly specified. He is insultingly referred to as a 'tortoise' (I.2.318), a 'fish' (II.2.25) and a 'beast' (IV.1.140), and in the final act Prospero describes him as 'This mis-shapen knave' (V.1.268) and as one who is 'as disproportion'd in his manners / As in his shape' (V.1.290–1). The people who describe him in these terms, however, have deliberately enslaved and debased him. We should be careful, therefore, about accepting such phrases

QUESTION

Some critics have described Prospero as a magnanimous ruler; others have claimed that he is a sadistic oppressive coloniser. Paying close attention to the text, offer your evaluation of his character. (Try not to be **anachronistic** in your views.)

CHECK THE BOOK

An excellent introduction to the subject of language being used to distort truth is Dwight Bolinger's *Language – The Loaded Weapon: The Use and Abuse of Language Today* (1990).

at face value. Debasing a person by the use of language is a well-known ploy of people who wish to subjugate others.

Much of what we know about his parentage and background comes from Prospero, who is prejudiced: 'Thou poisonous slave, got by the devil himself / Upon thy wicked dam' (I.2.321–2). Caliban is about twenty-four and had lived on the island for twelve years before the arrival of Prospero and Miranda. At first, Caliban says, he and Prospero were friends:

> When thou cam'st first
> Thou strok'st me, and made much of me; wouldst give me
> Water with berries in 't; and teach me how
> To name the bigger light, and how the less,
> That burn by day and night: and then I lov'd thee,
> And show'd thee all the qualities o' th' isle,
> The fresh springs, brine-pits, barren place and fertile …
> (I.2.334–40)

Caliban does not refute Prospero's claim that 'thou didst seek to violate / The honour of my child' (I.2.349–50). Rather, he regrets his lack of success: 'would 't had been done! / Thou didst prevent me; I had peopled else / This isle with Calibans' (I.2.351–3).

Even though Caliban has been enslaved by Prospero, he risks punishment by using the 'thou' form, normally only acceptable to inferiors or intimate equals, and his service is grudging because he regards Prospero as a usurper: 'This island's mine, by Sycorax my mother, / Which thou tak'st from me' (I.2.333–4). He plots with Stephano and Trinculo to kill Prospero:

> Why, as I told thee, 'tis a custom with him
> I' th' afternoon to sleep: there thou mayst brain him,
> Having first seiz'd his books; or with a log
> Batter his skull, or paunch him with a stake,
> Or cut his wezand with thy knife. (III.2.85–9)

Caliban shows considerable intelligence. He has learnt Prospero's language: 'You taught me language; and my profit on 't / Is, I know how to curse' (I.2.365–6) and is fully aware of the futility of arguing with one who has more power than he has: 'I must obey: his Art is of such pow'r, / It would control my dam's god, Setebos, / And make a vassal of him' (I.2.374–6).

Caliban has a better set of values than Stephano and Trinculo. They are distracted from their plan by their greed when they see Prospero's rich garments. Only Caliban realises that such finery is unimportant: 'Leave it alone, thou fool; it is but trash' (IV.1.224).

Caliban is sensitive to beauty and is given some of the most poetic lines in the play:

>   … the isle is full of noises,
> Sounds and sweet airs, that give delight, and hurt not.
> Sometimes a thousand twangling instruments
> Will hum about mine ears; and sometime voices,
> That, if I then had wak'd after long sleep,
> Will make me sleep again: and then, in dreaming,
> The clouds methought would open, and show riches
> Ready to drop upon me; that, when I wak'd,
> I cried to dream again. (III.2.133–41)

Caliban's motive for murder is less ignoble than that of Antonio and Sebastian. They plan to kill Alonso to gain his power and wealth; Caliban merely wants the return of 'his' island. You might like to think about whether Caliban's 'conversion' – 'I'll be wise hereafter, / And seek for grace' (V.1.294–5) – is likely or whether it is the result of tidying up all the strands in the **plot**. It seems probable that Caliban might be wiser in the future. He would certainly be less likely to be taken in by men such as Stephano and Trinculo.

Whatever you decide about Caliban, you will probably acknowledge that, in him, Shakespeare has created an unforgettable character. He is not perfect, any more than Shylock in *The Merchant of Venice* is perfect, but you may decide that they are 'More sinn'd against than sinning' (*King Lear*, III.2.60).

CHECK THE FILM

Watch Paul Mazursky's 1982 version of *The Tempest* and examine how it modifies your view of the characters. In particular, is Caliban portrayed as you think he should be?

ARIEL

As his name implies, Ariel is a spirit of the air. He is swift and delicate, ethereal and occasionally mischievous. 'Ariel' is a Hebrew name meaning 'lion of God', but perhaps he is more of a sprite than a lion. Shakespeare probably chose this name because it occurs occasionally in occult texts to mean a messenger between earth and the spirit world. Ariel is obedient to Prospero, and although he longs for his freedom he seems to take pleasure in his work:

> All hail, great master! grave sir, hail! I come
> To answer thy best pleasure; be 't to fly,
> To swim, to dive into the fire, to ride
> On the curl'd clouds, to thy strong bidding task
> Ariel and all his quality. (I.2.189–93)

He certainly deserves the freedom he asks for (I.2.245) because, as he reminds Prospero, he has never lied or cheated: 'Remember I have done thee worthy service; / Told thee no lies, made no mistakings, serv'd / Without grudge or grumblings' (I.2.247–9). It is interesting to contrast the terms of endearment applied to Ariel – 'my dainty Ariel', 'my bird', 'My Ariel, chick' – with the terms of opprobrium hurled at Caliban.

Although not human, Ariel is moved to pity by the plight of the royal party:

> Your charm so strongly works 'em,
> That if you now beheld them, your affections
> Would become tender.
> PROSPERO: Dost thou think so, spirit?
> ARIEL: Mine would, sir, were I human. (V.1.17–20)

One of Ariel's key roles in *The Tempest* is to provide music. His melodies are heard throughout the island and they can control the actions of the characters. Caliban is frequently lulled by airs 'that give delight' (III.2.134), and Ferdinand is lured to his meeting with Miranda by Ariel's music. You may agree that Ariel's nature excites the audience's admiration and that his music gives pleasure, but does his character lack the depth and complexity of Caliban's?

CHECK THE BOOK
Over the centuries numerous writers have identified the name of 'Ariel' with poetic imagination. Sylvia Plath's 'Ariel' is one example, while T. S. Eliot called five of his Christmas poems 'Ariel poems'.

CHECK THE NET
For a copy of Sylvia Plath's poem 'Ariel', see **http:// cityhonors. buffalo.k12.ny.us/ city/rsrcs/eng/ plasmi.html**

MIRANDA

Miranda is the only woman in the play. Her name is the equivalent of 'the wonderful one' or 'the one who causes admiration', and is **symbolic** of her beauty, innocence and modesty. When the play opens Miranda is almost fifteen, and for the previous twelve years she has lived on the island and has known only Prospero and Caliban. All who know Miranda are impressed by her beauty. Ferdinand thinks she is so lovely that she must be a goddess: 'Most sure the goddess / On whom these airs attend!' (I.2.424–5).

Miranda feels sympathy for the suffering of others. Indeed, the first words attributed to her in the play are an expression of her concern for those involved in the shipwreck:

> If by your Art, my dearest father, you have
> Put the wild waters in this roar, allay them.
> The sky, it seems, would pour down stinking pitch,
> But that the sea, mounting to th' welkin's cheek,
> Dashes the fire out. O, I have suffered
> With those that I saw suffer! (I.2.1–6)

She shows sympathy for everyone in pain except Caliban, whom she dislikes because he attempted to rape her, and she tries to avoid seeing him: ''Tis a villain, sir, / I do not love to look on' (I.2.311–12).

Miranda falls in love at first sight and she has the simplicity and forthrightness to express her love openly. Shortly after meeting Ferdinand she tells him: 'I am your wife if you will marry me; / If not, I'll die your maid' (III.1.83–4). The same quality of directness is shown in her open admiration of the attractive men in the courtly party: 'How many goodly creatures are there here! / How beauteous mankind is! O brave new world, / That has such people in 't!' (V.1.182–4). Yet, in spite of the immediacy of Miranda's love for Ferdinand, it seems to be a love that will endure, and it is certainly a generous love. When Miranda sees Ferdinand carrying logs, she is eager to share his labour and tells him: 'If you'll sit down, / I'll bear your logs the while: pray give me that; / I'll carry it to the pile' (III.1.23–5).

CHECK THE BOOK

It may be useful to compare Miranda with Perdita in *The Winter's Tale*. The two have much in common: youth, isolation from their peers and lack of knowledge of their position in society. They both fall in love with a young man who turns out to be a prince, and they both make the first moves in the relationship. Perhaps Shakespeare felt that their isolation from society saved them from artifice and coyness.

QUESTION

Discuss the suggestion that Miranda's character does not develop during the course of the play.

Miranda is beautiful, sympathetic, a character without blemish or artifice. You can judge for yourself whether such an idealisation of womanhood makes a heroine that we can identify with. There is, perhaps, one dissenting note that should be mentioned in our evaluation of Miranda. In Act I, Scene 2, the speech beginning 'Abhorred slave' is attributed to Miranda in early texts (lines 353–64). It is, however, so virulently cruel and so unlike many of her other utterances that many modern editors change the attribution and give the speech to Prospero. The Arden edition, which is used in these Notes, remains true to early versions, and gives this speech to Miranda.

FERDINAND

Ferdinand is handsome, courageous and honourable. His good looks impress Miranda so much that she thinks he is a spirit, albeit a fine-looking one: 'I might call him / A thing divine; for nothing natural / I ever saw so noble' (I.2.420–2). His courage in adversity is suggested by Francisco, who saw him jump into the sea and swim towards the island: 'I saw him beat the surges under him, / And ride upon their backs; he trod the water, / Whose enmity he flung aside' (II.1.110–12), and he bravely attempts to withstand imprisonment by Prospero: 'I will resist such entertainment till / Mine enemy has more pow'r' (I.2.468–9).

Ferdinand is a loving son. He grieves for the father he believes he has lost and describes himself as one: 'Who with mine eyes, never since at ebb, beheld / The King my father wrack'd (I.2.438–9). His love for Miranda is instantaneous but sincere and profound. He is willing to give up his throne and his country for her: 'Let me live here ever; / So rare a wonder'd father and a wise / Makes this place Paradise' (IV.1.122–4). His love is gentle and protective. He is touched when Miranda offers to share his labour but will not let her suffer on his behalf:

> No, precious creature;
> I had rather crack my sinews, break my back,
> Than you should such dishonour undergo,
> While I sit lazy by. (III.1.25–8)

CONTEXT

In Shakespeare's day the name Ferdinand might well have suggested Ferdinand of Aragon (1452–1516), the Spanish ruler who, with his wife Isabella, supported the voyage of Christopher Columbus in 1492 and who captured Granada from the Moors in the same year.

QUESTION

Is the love between Ferdinand and Miranda based on anything more than physical attraction? Examine their interaction and indicate whether such a love is likely to survive.

Ferdinand is perhaps an idealised example of romantic youth but he is not naive. He tells Miranda that he has had other experiences of women and, like many young bridegrooms, he is eager for the wedding night to come.

ALONSO

Alonso, the king of Naples, has sinned in the past, but he shows himself to be capable of remorse and to have a keen desire to repent. His crime against Prospero was inspired by Antonio, but he showed weakness in succumbing to Antonio's temptation, and cruelty in allowing Prospero and Miranda to be 'Expos'd unto the sea' (III.3.71).

Alonso is shown to have a number of redeeming qualities. He loves his son deeply and is grieved by his disappearance: 'O thou mine heir / Of Naples and of Milan, what strange fish / Hath made his meal on thee?' (II.1.107–9). So, in spite of fatigue, he searches the island for him: 'let's make further search / For my poor son' (II.1.318–19). Alonso is capable of inspiring devotion in his followers. Gonzalo loves him and defends him against Sebastian's criticism:

> My lord Sebastian,
> The truth thou speak doth lack some gentleness,
> And time to speak it in: you rub the sore,
> When you should bring the plaster. (II.1.132–5)

When Alonso is condemned by Ariel for his crimes against Prospero and Miranda, his conscience is pricked to such an extent that he thinks of committing suicide:

>   O, it is monstrous, monstrous!
> Methought the billows spoke, and told me of it;
> The winds did sing it to me; and the thunder,
> That deep and dreadful organ-pipe, pronounc'd
> The name of Prosper: it did bass my trespass.
> Therefor my son i' th' ooze is bedded; and
> I'll seek him deeper than e'er plummet sounded,
> And with him there lie mudded. (III.3.95–102)

QUESTION

Examine the care with which Prospero arranges his daughter's marriage with the information provided on Alonso's daughter. Take into account the fact that our main sources of information for the latter are Antonio and Sebastian, neither of whom can be regarded as trustworthy.

CHECK THE NET

For short critical comments and observations on *The Tempest* by esteemed authors such as Samuel Johnson (1709–84) and William Hazlitt (1778–1830), see **http://www. geocities.com/ litpageplus/ shakmoul- tempest.html**

You might like to ask yourself if there is any justice in the claims made by Antonio and Sebastian (II.1.119–31) that Alonso had sacrificed his daughter for the sake of a profitable alliance. You might wonder if his remorse is solely because he had wronged Prospero.

GONZALO

Gonzalo is described by Prospero as a 'noble Neapolitan' (I.2.161). He is an old man who is well intentioned and talkative. You might like to compare him with Polonius in *Hamlet*, a character that, according to tradition, Shakespeare himself played. Antonio mocks the old man's garrulity (II.1.258–60), claiming that his 'prating' is long-winded and of no value. His statements provide a commentary on the various incidents in the **plot**, from the shipwreck to the discovery of Ferdinand and Miranda. His remarks are usually optimistic and he seems cheerful even in the midst of disaster. In the first scene of the play, for example, he assures the others that they will not drown because the Boatswain has the appearance of a man who will hang: 'I have great comfort from this fellow: methinks he hath no drowning mark upon him; his complexion is perfect gallows' (I.1.28–30).

Gonzalo has been loyal to Alonso for at least twelve years. It is worth remembering that he is a Neapolitan and thus a subject of Alonso and not of Prospero. His sense of justice, however, persuaded him to treat Prospero and Miranda with kindness and so he provided them with 'Rich garments, linens, stuffs and necessaries' (I.2.164), as well as with food, water and books from Prospero's library. His continued loyalty to Alonso is shown in his reproach to Sebastian: 'My lord Sebastian, / The truth you speak doth lack some gentleness' (II.1.132–3). Prospero praises the old man's loyalty and perhaps sums up the audience's reaction to a likeable, loyal, talkative and cheerful nobleman: 'O good Gonzalo, / My true preserver, and a loyal sir / To him thou follow'st!' (V.1.68–70).

Shakespeare gives Gonzalo the task of expressing views on the ideal state or commonwealth. You might wonder why he is the chosen vehicle for the interesting (if misguided) views on an earthly utopia.

ANTONIO

Antonio is Prospero's brother. Prospero loved and trusted him but Antonio proved false: 'My brother, and thy uncle, call'd Antonio … he whom next thyself / Of all the world I lov'd' (I.2.66–9). Antonio is a pragmatist. He made an arrangement with Alonso, king of Naples, to deprive Prospero of his dukedom, and pays a yearly levy to the king. According to Prospero, Antonio would have killed Miranda and himself but he was afraid the people would not tolerate such an action since 'So dear the love my people bore me' (I.2.141).

Antonio seems to have lived well since Prospero's banishment and he was on sufficiently good terms with the king to be invited to the wedding of Alonso's daughter in Tunis. He does not seem to have suffered from a guilty conscience for his action towards Prospero. When Sebastian suggests that his conscience may have pricked him he replies: 'if 'twere a kibe, / 'Twould put me to my slipper: but I feel not / This deity in my bosom' (II.1.271–3). Antonio tempts Sebastian to kill his brother, Alonso, and actually offers to perform the action:

> Here lies your brother,
> No better than the earth he lies upon,
> If he were that which now he's like, that's dead;
> Whom I, with this obedient steel, three inches of it,
> Can lay to bed for ever … (II.1.275–9)

He knows human nature well and suggests that the majority of men will follow the person who has the power, irrespective of how he got it. Nevertheless, he is aware that Gonzalo is sincerely loyal to Alonso and so advises Sebastian to kill him.

Antonio has a sense of humour, as is shown in his witty exchanges with Sebastian in the first part of Act II, Scene 1, yet it is a cruel sense of humour, taking pleasure in mocking the talkativeness of an old man and rubbing salt in Alonso's wounds. In spite of all his weaknesses, however, Antonio has courage. He is as disturbed as the others by the disappearance of the banquet in Act III, Scene 3,

QUESTION

Examine the suggestion that Antonio is amoral rather than immoral. Is there any justification for his actions? (Before making a final decision, you might like to examine the theory of the divine right of kings. The Stuart kings believed absolutely in such a theory and *The Tempest* was performed at the court of James I.)

CITY AND ISLINGTON
SIXTH FORM COLLEGE
283 - 309 GOSWELL ROAD
LONDON

and as frightened as they are by Ariel's apparition, and yet he is prepared to follow Sebastian and fight the spirits (III.3.103).

Antonio shows no sign whatsoever of having repented any of his crimes and yet he is included in Prospero's general absolution:

> For you, most wicked sir, whom to call brother
> Would even infect my mouth, I do forgive
> Thy rankest faults, – all of them; and require
> My dukedom of thee, which perforce, I know,
> Thou must restore. (V.1.130–4)

CHECK THE BOOK

You might like to ask yourself if Antonio's character has been influenced by the ideas in Niccolò Machiavelli's *The Prince* (written 1513, published 1532).

You might like to think about the fact that Antonio neither thanks Prospero for his forgiveness nor comments on the loss of the dukedom. Indeed, he does not utter more than a few words for the rest of the play. Perhaps he has received the hardest punishment an ambitious man can receive: the loss of the temporal power he has fought so hard to attain.

SEBASTIAN

Sebastian is Alonso's brother and his friendship with Antonio suggests the nature of his character. Like Antonio, he mocks Gonzalo (II.1.11–100), and an indication of the ungenerous nature of such repartee is the fact that the passage is in prose not verse.

Sebastian seems to have been involved in Prospero's banishment, though his exact role is not indicated. Ariel criticises him in the same terms that he applies to Alonso and Antonio: 'You are three men of sin' (III.3.53) and 'you three / From Milan did supplant good Prospero' (III.3.69–70). Sebastian immediately succumbs to Antonio's temptation to kill Alonso, promising Antonio a reward for his services:

>   Thy case, dear friend,
> Shall be my precedent; as thou got'st Milan,
> I'll come by Naples. Draw thy sword: one stroke
> Shall free thee from the tribute which thou payest;
> And I the King shall love thee. (II.1.285–9)

Sebastian has courage. When Ariel and his spirits disappear, he is prepared to follow them and fight them one by one: 'But one fiend at a time, / I'll fight their legions o'er' (III.3.102–3). Like Antonio, he shows little sign of repentance and yet is included in Prospero's forgiveness. He also seems more willing to accept the fact that his plot has failed and to make the best of the situation. He rejoices (or appears to rejoice) in Ferdinand's discovery – 'A most high miracle!' (V.1.177) – and joins in the amused criticism of Stephano. Shakespeare leaves us in no doubt that Sebastian is an evil man, but perhaps his evil may be said to be triggered by Antonio rather than to come from any obvious personal predisposition towards sinfulness.

STEPHANO

Stephano is Alonso's butler and he is shown to be a totally self-interested opportunist. He plays a minor role but provides much of the humour of the play and acts as a contrast to the courtly characters, on one side; and to Caliban, on the other. He and Trinculo have not the status of Antonio or Sebastian but their characters are similar. They want more than they have a right to. Unlike Caliban, they do not want to kill Prospero to right a wrong, but merely as a means to financial reward.

TRINCULO

Trinculo is Alonso's jester and his role in the play is to provide some of the coarse humour that was a feature of the theatre of the time. He was probably dressed in a multicoloured garment, which would have informed the audience of his position. His character is not subtly drawn or clearly distinguishable from Stephano's. He is greedy, seeing Caliban as a potential source of future income, and willing to contemplate murder for financial gain. He is not interested in justice, but merely in getting as much as he can when the opportunity arises. He is forgiven for his crimes, although we may wonder if he shows any signs of penitence.

THE SUPERNATURAL

Although not a character in the conventional sense, it could be argued that the supernatural, in the form of gods, nymphs, naiads, strange creatures and unnatural weather phenomena, is as much a

CHECK THE BOOK

You might like to look at some of the areas of interest and disagreement to contemporary critics. Such areas include characterisation (especially of Prospero and Miranda), colonisation (especially the attitudes expressed by and at Caliban), the use of magical powers, and the role and suitability of **masques**.

character in the play as any of the humans. You could certainly argue that the supernatural has a profound impact on the characters and the themes of the play.

RECURRING THEMES

There are many recurrent themes in *The Tempest*, the most marked of which are the following. Some of the comments here are posed as questions to allow you to make up your own mind about the significance of the theme.

GOD AND HUMANITY

You might like to ask yourself if the play is an **allegory**. Certainly others have seen it in this light. In volume 3 of *Shakespeare Once More, Prose Works*, published between 1868 and 1890, James Russell Lowell (1819–91) wrote of *The Tempest*:

> If I read it rightly, it is an example of how a great poet should write allegory, – not embodying metaphysical abstractions, but giving us ideals abstracted from life itself, suggesting an under-meaning everywhere, forcing it upon us nowhere, tantalizing the mind with hints that imply so much and tell so little, and yet keep the attention all eye and ear with eager, if fruitless, expectation. Here the leading characters are not merely typical but symbolical, – that is, they do not illustrate a class of persons, they belong to universal Nature.

If it is allegorical, does Prospero represent God? It has been suggested that the island can be seen as the Garden of Eden; that Prospero, Miranda and Ariel are an allegorical representation of the Trinity, like Father, Daughter and Spirit. If Prospero is a godlike figure, is he a god of power or of love? To many modern readers he appears as an example of, at best, omniscient paternalism; at worst, a cruel manipulator. Was the usurping of Prospero by his brother a recasting of the story of Lucifer's battle against God, as in Genesis or in John Milton's *Paradise Lost*, or does it retell the Cain and Abel narrative or Esau's loss of his birthright to Jacob? Or is it more likely that it is a comment on the usurping of Richard III's throne

CONTEXT

You might like to examine the family tree of the rulers of England from Richard III to James I. The intricate relationships may shed some light on certain aspects of the play.

by Henry VII, the grandfather of Elizabeth I? Richard was killed at the Battle of Bosworth Field in 1485 and it was this battle that made Henry Tudor king. Since James I could claim descent from the same family as Richard III, it might have appeared that James was taking over a throne usurped by Henry Tudor.

LOVE

How many kinds of love do we find? Parent to child? Child to parent? Woman to man? Brother to brother? Master to slave? Courtier to king? Why are they introduced? Are there really only two strong expressions of love in the play? Are these Caliban's love of his island and the strong physical attraction between Miranda and Ferdinand?

MAGIC

Magic was something that was taken very seriously by people who lived in Europe at the time of Shakespeare. It is worth remembering that witches were still being burnt at the stake in the reign of James I. You might consider whether magic is ever used benignly in the play. (Think about Sycorax's imprisonment of Ariel, and Prospero's enslavement of Caliban and his insistence on unquestioning service from Ariel.) The tempest with which the play opens is the result of Prospero's control of the elements. It is true that no one was actually hurt by the experience, but everyone involved in it suffered, at least for a time. You might like to think about the fact that the **plot** of *The Tempest* is unlike many of Shakespeare's other plays in that it depends almost entirely on the use of supernatural powers. In *Macbeth*, for example, the witches may have an influence on the hero's behaviour, but he has free will and is thus capable of determining his own actions. This is not true of *The Tempest*, however, where the destiny of everyone from Prospero to Ariel, from Alonso to Caliban, is decided by supernatural intervention rather than by their characters or their actions. It is, of course, important to stress that in Shakespeare's time there was widespread belief in the power of magic. Part of this belief was the result of living in a harsh society where education was limited to the few and where there often seemed no natural explanation for events. An additional point worthy of some consideration is that certain places were associated with magic: wells, crossroads, hawthorn groves.

> **CONTEXT**
>
> In 1604 James I passed a statute against witches, tightening up and making more severe the laws against witchcraft. In it he decreed that anyone who 'shall use, practice, or exercise any witchcraft, enchantment, charm, or sorcery, whereby any person shall be killed, destroyed, wasted, consumed, pined, or lamed in his or her body, or any part thereof; that then every such offender or offenders, their aiders, abettors, and counselors, being of any the said offenses duly and lawfully convicted and attainted, shall suffer pains of death as a felon or felons, and shall lose the privilege and benefit of clergy and sanctuary'.

CONTEXT

Jawaharlal Nehru
(1889–1964)
expressed his view
on the subject in
this way: 'Life is
like a game of
cards. The hand
that is dealt you
represents
determinism; the
way you play it is
free will.'

In *The Tempest* the entire island has strong associations with the supernatural. Caliban's mother, Sycorax, a renowned witch, was banished there; Ariel and the other spirits belong on the island; Prospero's magical powers seem to have developed only after he reached it, and they are given up before he leaves. It is as if the island is enchanted. As Caliban says:

> ... the isle is full of noises,
> Sounds and sweet airs, that give delight, and hurt not.
> Sometimes a thousand twangling instruments
> Will hum about mine ears; and sometime voices,
> That, if I then had wak'd after long sleep,
> Will make me sleep again: and then, in dreaming,
> The clouds methought would open, and show riches
> Ready to drop upon me; that, when I wak'd,
> I cried to dream again. (III.2.133–41)

NATURE AND NURTURE

Could we not say that Prospero's attempt to nurture Caliban had failed because the nurture was meant to control him and not to free him? Is it true that Caliban is the only character that truly understands and loves nature, as it is represented in the play? Perhaps we might ask if the play is about heredity and environment. It certainly touches on these subjects, but brothers brought up in the same environment have markedly different characters; Miranda appears to have relatively little in common with her father or with Caliban, the only other person brought up on the island. Many believe that our character is determined by our genes (nature), while others claim that nurture explains all our actions and predispositions. To behaviourists, who hold the latter view, when a child is born it is like a tabula rasa, or blank surface, on which people, events and experiences are imprinted. Perhaps the play suggests that nature and nurture contribute to an individual's character and behaviour.

NEW WORLD AND OLD WORLD

Is the 'new' world of the island preferable to the 'old' world of Naples? If this is so, why does Miranda refer to the latter as 'O brave new world' (V.1.183)? (You might like to compare

CHECK THE NET

Use a search engine to study the current views on nurture and nature. How similar are they to the views expressed in *The Tempest*?

the island in *The Tempest* with the forest in *As You Like It*.)
Shakespeare's play was written at a time when European colonial
expansionism had brought to Europe stories of strange new worlds
and civilisations. Whereas many people assumed that Europeans
had a perfect right to go to countries in Asia, Africa and the
Americas, some people worried that 'civilisation' might not be
totally beneficial to all those contacted. Nevertheless, when you
are evaluating *The Tempest*, it is important to remember the time
when it was written and the beliefs and attitudes that were held
then. James I, for example, believed in the divine right of kings.
According to this view, kings were 'appointed' by God in that God
had ordained the rank into which an individual was born. If a king
was bad, then that was God's punishment on a group of people.
The Stuarts believed that no one had the right to usurp an ordained
king. (In view of this belief, it is perhaps ironic that the only two
monarchs ever executed in England were Mary Queen of Scots,
James I's mother; and Charles I, James I's son.)

POWER

Power is certainly thematic in the play, whether it is the power
of the elements or Prospero's control of them. Is it possible that
Shakespeare is questioning the use or value of political power?
Are we shown that its use by Prospero does not give him absolute
satisfaction and that it does not actually change the nature of either
Caliban or Ariel? What are we shown about the desire for power as
illustrated by Antonio and Sebastian at one level, and Stephano and
Trinculo at another? Is there any evidence that a benign use of power
involves responsibility? Is Gonzalo's commonwealth an ideal?

RECONCILIATION

At one level, the play deals with the subject of reconciliation
through repentance and forgiveness. Yet we might ask a number
of questions about this. Is Prospero truly reconciled to life on the
island? If not, why not? Are his efforts on the island geared towards
utilising the island's resources or regaining his dukedom? Is he fully
reconciled to his brother? More to the point, perhaps, is Antonio
reconciled to Prospero or will he want to be duke of Milan again? Is
Caliban reconciled to the morality of Prospero in spite of his final
words? Does the play illustrate any serious change of character?

**CHECK
THE NET**
Go to **http://www.
literatureclassics.
com/essays/167/**
for an essay entitled
'Four Sides of the
Circle: Aspects of
The Tempest' by Dr
Michael Evenden.

CHECK THE BOOK

Job 38:8 reads: 'Or who shut up the sea with doors, when it brake forth, as if it had issued out of the womb?'; Psalm 107:25, 28 reads: 'For he commandeth, and raiseth the stormy wind, which lifteth up the waves thereof ... Then they cry unto the Lord in their trouble, and he bringeth them out of their distresses.'

Perhaps we can excuse this by remembering the shortness of time during which the action occurs.

THE TEMPEST

You might like to think about the relevance of the theme of the tempest, a theme that has had, for millennia, spiritual as well as physical significance. Judaism, Christianity and Islam all frequently use readings associated with storms. In modern Christian liturgy, for example, services often combine a reading from the book of Job with a psalm and the story of Christ calming the waters (see Job 38:1, 8–11, 25, 35 and Psalm 107:23–5, 28–9).

MASQUES

Finally, we should point out how often, in his plays, Shakespeare uses a play within a play. In *The Tempest* we have the **masque** and the masque-like sequence of the banquet; in a play such as *Hamlet* we have the play that was intended to prove Claudius's guilt. You might like to consider whether the masques help to create an atmosphere of awe and power, or whether they distract from the main dramatic themes. Certainly music plays a bigger role in *The Tempest* than in most of Shakespeare's other work. You could consider why the play, like the island, is full of music.

QUESTION

Read some of the information available on the dramatic unities. Why do you think dramatists chose to write within such restrictions? Are the gains sufficient to compensate for the loss of naturalism?

THE HANDLING OF TIME

The treatment of time causes two major problems in *The Tempest*. Because Shakespeare adheres to the classical **unities** (see **Dramatic unities**), much of the information required by the audience has to be provided by narration rather than by action. Thus, most of the history of Antonio's treachery to his brother is provided in Prospero's long account in Act I, Scene 2 under the pretext of telling Miranda about her past. It is undoubtedly a mark of Shakespeare's skill that he can incorporate so much background information into a reasonably naturalistic scene. Even then, he breaks it up for both Miranda and the audience by bringing in Ariel with his account of the shipwreck.

The second temporal problem relates to the compression of events. In the space of approximately four hours, the audience is asked to 'believe' that the following events have taken place:

- A shipwreck has occurred.

- Ferdinand meets and falls in love with Miranda, and has the time to carry logs and convince Prospero that his feelings for Miranda are genuine.

- Antonio and Sebastian plot the murder of Alonso.

- Caliban, Trinculo and Stephano plot the murder of Prospero.

- Alonso undergoes a conversion and repents for his crime against Prospero.

- A marriage is arranged.

- The plotters are forgiven.

- Ariel is freed and Caliban left in control of his island.

- The ship is found to be seaworthy and the party prepares to leave the island.

In your analysis of the play, you must ask yourself if the speed with which the audience is carried along makes us overlook such temporal improbabilities. Is the time scheme any more unlikely in *The Tempest* than in *Othello* or *The Winter's Tale*? When we go to the theatre, are we not conditioned to accept the constraints of time imposed by the writer? Do we not, in Samuel Taylor Coleridge's phrase, 'willingly suspend our disbelief'?

LANGUAGE AND STYLE

Every living language changes. Differences in pronunciation and in linguistic preferences are often apparent even in the speech of parents and their children, so it is not surprising that the language of Shakespeare's plays should be markedly different from the English we use almost four centuries later. In the sixteenth century, the English language was only beginning to be used by creative writers.

 CHECK THE BOOK

For anyone who would like to know more about Shakespeare's language, Norman Blake's *The Language of Shakespeare* (1989) is a useful starting point. It is not, however, for the faint-hearted.

Previously, Latin and French had been considered more suitable for literary expression than English, and consequently the English language had not been as fully developed as it later became.

The main differences between Shakespearean and modern English can, for convenience, be considered under such categories as mobility of word classes, vocabulary loss, verb forms, pronouns, prepositions, multiple negation and spelling and punctuation.

MOBILITY OF WORD CLASSES

Adjectives, nouns and verbs were less rigidly confined to their specific classes in Shakespeare's day. Adjectives were often used as adverbs. In V.1.309 Prospero describes the lovers as 'our dear-belov'd', where modern standard usage would require 'our dearly beloved'. Adjectives could also be used as nouns. In I.2.329 Prospero speaks of 'that vast of night', where today we would prefer 'vastness' or perhaps 'vast abyss'. Nouns were often used as verbs. In I.2.344 Caliban complains: 'and here you sty me', where the noun 'sty' is used as if it were a verb with the meaning of 'keep me in a filthy place'. Verbs were also, on occasion, used as nouns. In I.2.70, for example, when Prospero explains that he had neglected his prime duty by entrusting to his brother, Antonio, 'The manage of my state', the verb 'manage' is used in a context where we would today need 'management'.

CHANGES IN WORD MEANING

Words change their meanings as time passes, and so many words used by Shakespeare have different values today. Such semantic changes can be illustrated by the following examples:

Word	Meaning in the play	Current meaning	Reference
admire	wonder at	look at with pleasure	V.1.154
complexion	outward appearance	facial colouring	I.1.29
engine	instrument of war	machine	II.1.157

VOCABULARY LOSS

One of the difficulties faced by a member of a contemporary audience is the fact that many of the words used by the playwright are no longer current in modern English. For example:

CHECK THE NET

There is some very useful information on Shakespeare's London at **http://www.britannia.com/hiddenlondon/shakespeare.html**

Word	Meaning in the play	Reference
bombard	a vessel used for carrying liquids	II.2.21
bootless	useless, without value	I.2.35
bosky	covered and shaded by trees	IV.1.81
chough	jackdaw	II.1.261
doit	small coin worth about a halfpenny	II.2.32

VERB FORMS

Shakespearean verb forms differ from modern usage in three main ways. First, questions and negatives could be formed without using 'do' or 'did'. Thus in II.1.311 Alonso asks Gonzalo: 'Heard you this, Gonzalo?', where today one would have to say: 'Did you hear this, Gonzalo?' Similarly, in II.1.272–3 Antonio says: 'but I feel not / This deity in my bosom', using a construction that would be considered ungrammatical in modern English. We must add, however, that Shakespeare often formed questions and negatives as we do today. In I.1.13, for example, the Boatswain asks: 'Do you not hear him?' and in I.2.40 Prospero tells Miranda: 'I do not think thou canst'. Summing up, we can say that whereas Shakespeare could use both the A and B forms shown below, modern English permits only the B structures.

A	B
Like you it?	Do you like it?
I like it not.	I do not like it.
Liked you it?	Did you like it?
I liked it not.	I did not like it.

Secondly, some past tense forms are used which would be ungrammatical today. Among the many examples to be found are the following:

Form in the play	Current form	Reference
blessedly help hither	blessedly helped here	I.2.63
Hast thou forgot ...?	Have you forgotten?	I.2.257
I have broke your hest	I have broken your command	III.1.37
my enemies are all knit up	my enemies are all knitted up	III.3.89
Fairly spoke	Fairly spoken	IV.1.31

CHECK THE NET http://www. revision- notes.co.uk is a site that offers different levels of help with study and revision. The help on offer is generally of a high standard but must be evaluated and assimilated before being used.

Thirdly, archaic forms of the verb occur with the pronoun 'thou' and, on occasion, with the pronouns 'he', 'she' and 'it', for example: 'Thou didst smile' (I.2.153) and 'he hath lost his fellows' (I.2.419).

PRONOUNS

Shakespeare's pronoun usage differs to some extent from our own. There was a certain amount of choice in the use of second person pronouns in Elizabethan English. 'You' had to be used when addressing more than one person. The Boatswain uses it when rebuking the royal party: 'Do you not hear him? You mar our labour: keep your cabins' (I.1.13–14). 'You' also had to be used when a speaker wished to indicate respect. Thus Miranda and Ferdinand show their mutual respect by addressing each other as 'you':

MIRANDA: Do you love me?
FERDINAND: O heaven, O earth, bear witness to this sound,
    And crown what I profess with kind event,
    If I speak true! if hollowly, invert
    What best is boded me to mischief! I,
    Beyond all limit of what else i' th' world,
    Do love, prize, honour you. (III.1.67–73)

Superiors often used 'thou' to their inferiors and were, in return, addressed as 'you'. Gonzalo, for example, tells the Boatswain: 'Good, yet remember whom thou hast aboard' (I.1.19), to which the Boatswain replies: 'None that I more love than myself. You are a counsellor; if you can command these elements to silence, and work the peace of the presence, we will not hand a rope more' (I.1.20–3). The use of 'thou' could, depending on the situation, indicate that the speaker was talking to an intimate and so, as we would expect, it is the form used by Prospero when speaking to Miranda: 'I have done nothing but in care of thee, / Of thee, my dear one; thee, my daughter' (I.2.16–17). When used inappropriately, however, 'thou' could imply an insult.

One further pronominal difference which may be noted is the use of 'it' to refer to a person. In I.2.311 Miranda describes Caliban thus: ''Tis a villain, sir'; and in III.2.101 Stephano uses 'it' to refer to Miranda: 'Is it so brave a lass?'

CHECK THE BOOK

Read Angus McIntosh's article 'As You Like It: a grammatical clue to character'. It shows how a study of the use of 'thou' and 'you' in a Shakespeare play can help our understanding of changing attitudes in characters. (See Patterns of Language: Papers in General, Descriptive and Applied Linguistics, edited by Angus McIntosh and M. A. K. Halliday, 1966.)

PREPOSITIONS

In Shakespeare's day prepositional usage was less standardised than it is now, and so many of the writer's prepositions differ from those we would employ today. Among these are:

Preposition in the play	Preferred modern usage	Reference
she was **of** Carthage	she was from Carthage	II.1.79
And suck'd my verdure out **on** 't	And sucked my health out of it	I.2.87
on a trice	in a trice, quickly	V.1.238
such a paragon **to** their Queen	such a paragon for their Queen	II.1.71–2
with a twink	in the twinkling of an eye	IV.1.43

MULTIPLE NEGATION

In contemporary English we normally use only one negative in a sentence, but in Shakespeare's day two or even more negatives could be used for emphasis. His sonnet 'Let me not to the marriage of true minds' (Sonnet 116), for example, concludes with the following couplet: 'If this be error and upon me proved, / I never writ, nor no man ever loved.'

In *The Tempest* we find many examples of double negatives, among them the following: 'This is **no** mortal business, **nor no** sound / That the earth owes' (I.2.409–10) and '**Nor** go **neither**; but you'll lie, like dogs, and yet say **nothing neither**' (III.2.18–19).

SPELLING AND PUNCTUATION

Contemporary spelling and punctuation are markedly different from Shakespeare's usage. This aspect of his work need not, however, detain us because almost all modern editions make use of contemporary conventions. To illustrate the differences, however, we shall quote a verse of the story of Babel from the King James **Bible** of 1611:

1611 version of Genesis 11:4	Contemporary version
And they said; Goe to, let vs build vs a city and a tower, whose top may reach vnto heauen, and let vs make vs a name, lest we be scattered abroad vpon the face of the whole earth.	And they said: 'So, let us build a city and a tower whose top will reach to the sky, and let us immortalise our name in case we are scattered far and wide.

 CHECK THE BOOK

Charles Barber in *The English Language: A Historical Introduction* gives an excellent survey of the history and development of the English language (2000).

Spelling and punctuation continued

 CHECK THE NET
There is some excellent information available in online articles from the *Encyclopaedia Britannica*. At **http://www. britannica.com/ eb/article? eu=108550**, for example, you will find interesting information on the development of the English language and on elegiac verse.

The style of *The Tempest* is reminiscent of several of Shakespeare's final plays. It includes poetry of great beauty and elegiac notes that might, in an earlier period, have produced a tragedy. It is not 'realistic' in the sense of giving the audience a clear idea of life in seventeenth-century England, but it raises issues that were, and are, relevant. We may criticise the unnaturalness of some of the episodes; we may worry about inconsistencies in characters and attitudes; but, like other pieces of great literature, it can evoke what William Wordsworth (1770–1850) called 'The still, sad music of humanity' ('Lines composed a few miles above Tintern Abbey').

IMAGERY AND SYMBOLISM

Creative writers enjoy considerable freedom in their use of language in that they can mould and manipulate it to suit their literary purposes. Poetic language derives from ordinary, everyday speech but differs from it in that its purpose is not merely to communicate facts but also to delight and impress its audience by exploiting the resources of the language to the full. Poetic language differs from literary prose in that it is often rhythmically regular. We can compare, for example, the regular stress pattern of Ariel's comment to Prospero:

> Not a hair perish'd;
> On their sustaining garments not a blemish,
> But fresher than before: and, as thou bad'st me.
> In troops I have dispers'd them 'bout the isle (I.2.217–20)

with the more speech-like prose statement of Stephano:

> ... Where the devil
> should he learn our language? I will give him some
> relief, if it be but for that. If I can recover him, and
> keep him tame, and get to Naples with him, he's a
> present for any emperor that ever trod on neat's-
> leather. (II.2.67–72)

It is probably true to say that *The Tempest* is more concerned
with the exploration of ideas, especially those associated with
sin, repentance and purgation, than with the development of
interlocking images. But the use of images is basic to all vivid
language and can occur in poetry and prose alike.

IMAGERY

In *The Tempest* we find recurrent images of the sea. For example:
'The sky, it seems, would pour down stinking pitch, / But that the
sea, mounting to th' welkin's cheek, / Dashes the fire out' (I.2.3–5),
and: '*Nothing of him that doth fade, / But doth suffer a sea-change
/ Into something rich and strange*' (I.2.402–4).

We also find a wide range of images connected with the body
(sometimes associated with the sea), especially the internal workings
of the body or the pains inflicted on it. For example:

> Thou dost, and think'st it much to tread the ooze
> Of the salt deep,
> To run upon the sharp wind of the north,
> To do me business in the veins o' th' earth
> When it is bak'd with frost. (I.2.252–6)

See also: 'You cram these words into mine ears against / The
stomach of my sense' (II.1.102–3), or, in Prospero's threats to
Caliban: 'For this, be sure, to-night thou shalt have cramps, / Side-
stitches that shall pen thy breath up' (I.2.327–8).

SIMILE AND METAPHOR

Both similes and **metaphors** are often found in literary language
because they allow the writer to extend the range of references.
If Shakespeare, for example, says that love is like war, or life is
like the sea, he can then use images of war and of the sea when
describing love and life. Similes and metaphors involve
comparisons. With similes the comparison is overt. We say that one
thing is like another or has some of the qualities of something else.
Thus Gonzalo uses a simile when he compares the guilt of the three
men of sin to poison: 'All three of them are desperate: their great

QUESTION

Comment on the
importance of
music (including
songs) in *The
Tempest*.

guilt, / Like poison given to work a great time after, / Now 'gins to bite the spirits' (III.3.104–6). Prospero uses another when he tells Ariel he will soon be free: 'Thou shalt be as free / As mountain winds' (I.2.501–2).

CHECK THE BOOK

Upon receiving the news of Lady Macbeth's death, Macbeth exclaims: 'Out, out, brief candle!' (V.5.23).

With a metaphor, the comparison is implied rather than stated. When, in *Macbeth*, Shakespeare writes that the brevity of life resembles the short existence of a candle which can be put out at any moment, he is using a metaphor. Metaphors are used in all varieties of language and numerous examples can be found in *The Tempest*. Gonzalo uses a metaphor when he personifies nature in a description of his ideal world:

> All things in common Nature should produce
> Without sweat or endeavour: treason, felony,
> Sword, pike, knife, gun, or need of any engine,
> Would I not have; but Nature should bring forth,
> Of it own kind, all foison, all abundance,
> To feed my innocent people. (II.1.155–60)

CHECK THE FILM

Stanislav Sokolov directed a delightful animated version of *The Tempest* in 1992. You may like to examine how he modified the text and how his animated characters match your own views on, say, Prospero, Miranda and Caliban.

There are three metaphors in Antonio's temptation speech, when he speaks of steel as if it could obey, when he compares death to an eternal wink and when Gonzalo is described as a morsel:

> Here lies your brother,
> No better than the earth he lies upon,
> If he were that which now he's like, that's dead;
> Whom I, with this obedient steel, three inches of it,
> Can lay to bed for ever; whiles you, doing thus,
> To the perpetual wink for aye might put
> This ancient morsel … (II.1.275–81)

WORDPLAY

Playing on different meanings of the same word or on words which sound alike has been popular in English literature since the time of Chaucer. Shakespeare and his contemporaries employed wordplay as a literary technique and also for the amusement and intellectual pleasure it seems to have given their audience. Examples of wordplay can be found throughout *The Tempest*, especially in the scenes which provide comic relief. We find it in Act I, Scene 2, for example, when Prospero utilises two meanings of 'key', an object which can open a door and the pitch of a melody: 'having both the key / Of officer and office, set all hearts i' th' state / To what tune pleas'd his ear' (lines 83–5).

Later, in III.1.83–6, Miranda plays on the two meanings of 'maid', a domestic servant and a virgin:

> I am your wife if you will marry me;
> If not, I'll die your maid: to be your fellow
> You may deny me; but I'll be your servant,
> Whether you will or no.

DRAMATIC IRONY

This term is applied to an episode in a play where the audience can see more significance in the words of a character than the other characters can. In I.2.463–7, for example, Miranda and Ferdinand take Prospero's criticisms at face value:

> Speak not you for him: he's a traitor. Come;
> I'll manacle thy neck and feet together:
> Sea-water shalt thou drink; thy food shall be
> The fresh-brook mussels, wither'd roots, and husks
> Wherein the acorn cradled.

However, the audience realises that Prospero has arranged the meeting between Ferdinand and his daughter in the hope that they will fall in love and thus heal the breach between Naples and Milan. The punishment is so that Ferdinand will not feel that Miranda is won too easily.

SYMBOLISM

When Shakespeare encourages us to see a character or an occurrence as representing another level of meaning, then he is making use of **symbolism**. It is a technique that allows him to express abstract ideas through physical **imagery**. The very title of this play is symbolic in that it suggests turbulent relationships as well as a

 QUESTION

Coleridge wrote: 'The whole courting scene ... between the two lovers is a masterpiece.' (See *Coleridge on Shakespeare. The Text of the Lectures of 1811–12*, edited R. A. Foakes, 1971.) Examine this scene, showing in what ways it could be considered a 'masterpiece'.

Symbolism continued

storm at sea; the animal imagery associated with Caliban may well be symbolic of Prospero's attitude to him; and the airs, both musical and physical, that are a feature of Ariel may suggest the spirit freed from physical limitations.

The language of *The Tempest* is less image-laden than many of Shakespeare's other dramas. Instead of a preponderance of images of decay, for example, that we find in *King Lear*, we find an interest in themes and ideas often underlined by the repetition of such key words as 'beauty', 'brave', 'nature', 'noble' and 'virtue'.

It has often been suggested that the **action** in *The Tempest* is not true to life, that the shipwreck, love affair and final reconciliation could not possibly have occurred in four hours. It is worth remembering, however, that a marriage ends a Shakespearean comedy or **tragicomedy** just as surely as deaths end a tragedy. In addition, one does not look to literature for chronological precision or logical exactness. The truth which has value in a work of art is a truth which imposes a coherence on the many narrative strands that are woven together by the artist.

 QUESTION

Do you think that *The Tempest* really is a tragicomedy? List the tragic and the comic possibilities and consider the fact that the audience is told as early as Act I, Scene 1 that no harm will come to anyone.

PART FOUR

CRITICAL HISTORY

RECEPTION AND EARLY CRITICAL VIEWS

We know more about the early reception of *The Tempest* than we do about many of Shakespeare's plays. It was first performed on 1 November 1611 in Whitehall in the presence of King James I. We do not have any records of how the play was received but the subject matter was topical (James I was interested in colonisation and had sponsored Sir Walter Raleigh's last trip to South America), and it was selected for another courtly performance in 1613 to celebrate the marriage of James I's daughter, Elizabeth, to Prince Frederick of Bohemia. When Shakespeare's works were collected and published in 1623, *The Tempest* appeared first, a fact that may suggest its popularity at the time. It has remained popular ever since, attracting not only audiences but painters too, including Richard Dadd, George Romney and Henry Townsend.

The **plot** of *The Tempest* may be divorced from real life in that its chief character, Prospero, is a magician who can control the spirits of air, earth, fire and water, and who can use spells to put Miranda to sleep, to punish Caliban and to remedy old wrongs. The play presupposes a knowledge of and interest in the supernatural, an interest that was probably more widespread in Shakespeare's day than in our own. It is worth noting, for example, that King James I wrote a treatise on magic in 1603. And yet, in spite of the unreality of the setting and of Prospero's mysterious powers, the play deals with themes like love, sin and repentance, and colonial contacts – themes that relate to the world of reality and have as much significance now as they had when Shakespeare wrote.

CRITICAL HISTORY

Shakespeare's plays, like all drama, fell out of favour during the Cromwellian period and there is no record of any production for half a century. In 1667 John Dryden (1631–1700) and William

> **CONTEXT**
>
> The date for *The Tempest* is fixed as 1610–11 by its performance at court and by Shakespeare's use of William Strachey's letter (dated 15 July 1610 from Virginia) of a shipwreck off the coast of Bermuda in 1609.

 CHECK THE NET

For an extract from William Strachey's letter *A True Reportory of the Wrack and Redemption of Sir Thomas Gates, Knight* (not published until its inclusion in *Purchas His Pilgrimes* in 1625), see **http:// arches.uga.edu/ ~iyengar/Strachey. html**

D'Avenant (1606–68) adapted *The Tempest* for a post-Restoration audience. Their version, *The Tempest; or, the Enchanted Island*, is a light-hearted comedy, lacking the depth and tragic elements of the original; but until the nineteenth century theirs was the preferred edition. They created a series of new characters so that Caliban and Ariel could have sexual partners; they gave Miranda and Caliban sisters, Dorinda and Sycorax respectively; and Prospero was given a ward, Hippolito, a young man who had never seen a woman. It was normal, too, for Ariel to be played as a female character. Indeed, this tradition lasted until the 1930s. The D'Avenant and Dryden adaptation was popularised further when Matthew Locke composed incidental instrumental music for *The Tempest*, and it was produced as an opera in 1667. It was not until 1838 that the original version began to be regularly performed again. D'Avenant and Dryden appealed to audiences by concentrating on the problems and humour associated with sexual jealousy, although they introduced a note of political satire in the quarrels between Stephano and Trinculo. You will get an idea of the difference in quality between Shakespeare's play and the D'Avenant–Dryden version by comparing Caliban's speech in I.2.343–6:

> For I am all the subjects that you have,
> Which first was mine own King: and here you sty me
> In this hard rock, whiles you do keep from me
> The rest o' th' island

with:

> for I am all the Subjects that thou hast. I first was mine own
> Lord; and here thou stay'st me in this hard Rock, whiles thou
> dost keep from me the rest o'th' Island.

In the early eighteenth century, *The Tempest* was regarded as a delightful but far-fetched fantasy, although many writers, including Joseph Addison (1672–1719) and Samuel Johnson (1709–84), were impressed by the depiction of Caliban and preferred the original text to the Dryden and D'Avenant version. Towards the second part of this century, **critics** began to comment on the romance and imaginative extravagance of the play, and the poet Samuel Taylor

CHECK THE NET
See **http://andromeda.rutgers.edu/~jlynch/Texts/tempest.html** for the full text of *The Tempest; or, The Enchanted Island* by John Dryden and William D'Avenant.

Coleridge (1772–1834) wrote several essays on it, suggesting that it was, in a very real sense, a dramatic poem whose themes were too profound to be understood properly from watching a performance.

In the nineteenth century, some performances were romantic and others delighted in the technical advances of the contemporary stage. The Charles Keane production of 1857 is an example of the latter. It was said to involve one hundred and forty workers nightly to operate the elaborate machinery and create the stage effects favoured by early Victorian theatregoers.

The New Shakespeare Society was founded in 1873 and, under its influence, attempts were made to produce the play as Shakespeare intended. Directors broke away from much of the technical extravaganza and staged *The Tempest* as a realistic drama rather than as a romantic poem. There was, however, a tendency to concentrate on an idealised maturity that stressed the value of wise old age.

Early twentieth-century critics such as Lytton Strachey tended to stress a cynical and disillusioned interpretation. They suggested that *The Tempest* failed to satisfy because it was the product of a jaded genius. In 1904, for example, in an essay entitled 'Shakespeare's Final Period', Strachey wrote that Shakespeare was:

> Bored with people, bored with real life, bored with drama, bored, in fact, with everything except poetry and poetical dreams. He is no longer interested, one often feels, in what happens, or who says what, so long as he can find a place for a faultless lyric, or a new, unimagined rhythmical effect, or a grand and mystic speech.

The second half of the twentieth century has seen a reappraisal of the play. Many productions reveal the power of the language, the subtlety of much of the characterisation, the richness of meaning and the complexity of the themes.

Throughout the period between Shakespeare's time and ours, however, few critics or audiences have failed to be impressed by the characters of Prospero and Caliban. Prospero may be depicted as a

CONTEXT

As well as inspiring many literary works, *The Tempest* has also inspired musical compositions, including Hector Berlioz's *Lélio* (1983), Jean Sibelius's incidental music for the play (first performed in Copenhagen in 1926) and Sir Michael Tippett's opera *The Knot Garden* (1969).

CHECK THE NET
A good source
of articles on
Shakespeare and
the theatre in
Britain can be found
at **http://www.
britishtheatre
guide.info/articles/
articleindex.htm**

godlike figure, meting out an ill-understood justice, or as a despotic coloniser; Caliban may be seen as an example of the Rousseauesque 'noble savage', or as a representative of a subjugated people, bound in body but free in spirit. Whatever interpretation a director chooses, the language allows for a degree of latitude. We can pick out certain characteristics but, even when we have listed them exhaustively, we still cannot pigeon-hole them because they are like real people in their ability to surprise us, even when we think we have plumbed their depths.

CONTEMPORARY APPROACHES

The Tempest resembles *The Merchant of Venice* in that modern audiences tend to react differently from Shakespeare's contemporaries to Caliban and Shylock. For us, living after colonisation and the Holocaust and aware of the dangers of prejudice, it is impossible not to sympathise with these characters, although there is evidence that many of Shakespeare's contemporaries would not have shared this sympathy. Perhaps, it is a tribute to Shakespeare's greatness as a dramatist and to his sensitivity as a person that the plays themselves allow us to empathise with both Caliban and Shylock.

PART FIVE

BACKGROUND

WILLIAM SHAKESPEARE'S LIFE

There are no personal records of Shakespeare's life. Official documents and occasional references to him by contemporary dramatists enable us to draw the main outline of his public life, but his private life remains hidden. Although not at all unusual for a writer of his time, this lack of first-hand evidence has tempted many to read his plays as personal records and to look in them for clues to Shakespeare's character and convictions. The results are unconvincing, partly because Renaissance art was not subjective or designed primarily to express its creator's personality, and partly because the drama of any period is very difficult to read biographically. Except when plays are written by committed dramatists to promote social or political causes (as by Shaw or Brecht), it is all but impossible to decide who amongst the variety of fictional characters in a drama represents the dramatist, or which of the various and often conflicting points of view expressed is authorial.

What we do know can be quickly summarised. Shakespeare was born into a well-to-do family in the market town of Stratford-upon-Avon in Warwickshire, where he was baptised, in Holy Trinity Church, on 26 April 1564. His father, John Shakespeare, was a prosperous glover and leather merchant who became a person of some importance in the town: in 1565 he was elected an alderman of the town, and in 1568 he became high bailiff (or mayor) of Stratford. In 1557 he had married Mary Arden. Their third child (of eight) and eldest son, William, learnt to read and write at the primary (or 'petty') school in Stratford and then, it seems probable, attended the local grammar school, where he would have studied Latin, history, logic and **rhetoric**. In November 1582 William, then aged eighteen, married Anne Hathaway, who was twenty-six years old. They had a daughter, Susanna, in May 1583, and twins, Hamnet and Judith, in 1585.

CHECK THE BOOK

There are a number of biographies of Shakespeare – many of them very speculative – but the most authoritative is still Samuel Schoenbaum's *Shakespeare: A Documentary Life* (1975).

Shakespeare next appears in the historical record in 1592 when he is mentioned as a London actor and playwright in a pamphlet by the dramatist Robert Greene. These 'lost years' 1585–92 have been the subject of much speculation, but how they were occupied remains as much a mystery as when Shakespeare left Stratford, and why. In his pamphlet, *Greene's Groatsworth of Wit*, Greene expresses to his fellow dramatists his outrage that the 'upstart crow' Shakespeare has the impudence to believe he 'is as well able to bombast out a blank verse as the best of you'. To have aroused this hostility from a rival, Shakespeare must, by 1592, have been long enough in London to have made a name for himself as a playwright. We may conjecture that he had left Stratford in 1586 or 1587.

 CHECK THE NET

You can read Shakespeare's will in his own handwriting – and in modern transcription – online at the Public Records Office: **http://www.pro. gov.uk/ virtualmuseum** and search for 'Shakespeare'.

During the next twenty years, Shakespeare continued to live in London, regularly visiting his wife and family in Stratford. He continued to act, but his chief fame was as a dramatist. From 1594 he wrote exclusively for the Lord Chamberlain's Men, which rapidly became the leading dramatic company and from 1603 enjoyed the patronage of James I as the King's Men. His plays were extremely popular and he became a shareholder in his theatre company. He was able to buy lands around Stratford and a large house in the town, to which he retired about 1611. He died there on 23 April 1616 and was buried in Holy Trinity Church on 25 April.

SHAKESPEARE'S DRAMATIC CAREER

Between the late 1580s and 1613 Shakespeare wrote thirty-seven plays, and contributed to some by other dramatists. This was by no means an exceptional number for a professional playwright of the times. The exact date of the composition of individual plays is a matter of debate – the date of first performance is known for only a few plays – but the broad outlines of Shakespeare's dramatic career have been established. He began in the late 1580s and early 1590s by rewriting earlier plays and working with plotlines inspired by the classics. He concentrated on comedies (such as *The Comedy of Errors*, 1590–4, which derived from the Latin playwright Plautus) and plays dealing with English history (such as the three parts of *Henry VI*, 1589–92), though he also tried his hand at bloodthirsty revenge tragedy (*Titus Andronicus*, 1592–3, indebted to both Ovid and Seneca). During the 1590s Shakespeare developed his expertise in these kinds of plays to write comic masterpieces such as *A Midsummer Night's Dream* (1594–5) and *As You Like It* (1599–1600), and history plays such as *Henry IV* (1596–8) and *Henry V* (1598–9).

As the new century begins a new note is detectable. Plays such as *Troilus and Cressida* (1601–2) and *Measure for Measure* (1603–4), poised between comedy and tragedy, evoke complex responses. Because of their **generic** uncertainty and ambivalent tone such works are sometimes referred to as 'problem plays', but it is tragedy which comes to dominate the extraordinary sequence of masterpieces: *Hamlet* (1600–1), *Othello* (1602–4), *King Lear* (1605–6), *Macbeth* (1605–6) and *Antony and Cleopatra* (1606).

In the last years of his dramatic career, Shakespeare wrote a group of plays of a quite different kind. These 'romances', as they are often called, are in many ways the most remarkable of all his plays. The group comprises *Pericles* (1608), *Cymbeline* (1609–11), *The Winter's Tale* (1610–11) and *The Tempest* (1610–11). These plays (particularly *Cymbeline*) reprise many of the situations and themes of the earlier dramas but in fantastical and exotic dramatic designs which, set in distant lands, covering large tracts of time and involving music, **mime**, dance and tableaux, have something of the qualities of **masques** and pageants. The situations which in the tragedies had led to disaster are here resolved: the great theme is restoration and reconciliation. Where in the tragedies Ophelia, Desdemona and Cordelia die, the daughters of these plays – Marina, Imogen, Perdita, Miranda – survive and are reunited with their parents and lovers.

THE TEXTS OF SHAKESPEARE'S PLAYS

Nineteen of Shakespeare's plays were printed during his lifetime in what are called 'quartos': books, each containing one play, and made up of sheets of paper each folded twice to make four leaves. Shakespeare, however, did not supervise their publication. This was not unusual. When a playwright sold a play to a dramatic company he sold his rights in it: copyright belonged to whoever had possession of an actual copy of the text, and consequently authors had no control over what happened to their work. Anyone who

CHECK THE FILM
There are lots of **anachronisms** and inaccuracies in *Shakespeare in Love* (1998) – that's half the fun of it – but its depiction of the hand-to-mouth world of the commercial theatre has something of the energy and edginess from which Shakespeare drew his artistic power.

CONTEXT
A **quarto** is a small format book, roughly equivalent to a modern paperback. Play texts in quarto form typically cost sixpence, as opposed to the cost of going to the theatre at a penny.

CONTEXT

Plays were not considered as serious literature in this period: when, in 1612, Sir Thomas Bodley was setting up his library in Oxford he instructed his staff not to buy any drama for the collection: 'haply [perhaps] some plays may be worthy the keeping, but hardly one in forty'.

CHECK THE NET

You can find out more about the earliest editions of Shakespeare at the University of Pennsylvania's ERIC site: **http://oldsite. library.upenn.edu/ etext/collections/ furness/eric/eric. html**

could get hold of the text of a play might publish it if they wished. Hence, what found its way into print might be the author's copy, but it might be an actor's copy or prompt copy, perhaps cut or altered for performance; sometimes actors (or even members of the audience) might publish what they could remember of the text. Printers, working without the benefit of the author's oversight, introduced their own errors, through misreading the manuscript, for example, and by 'correcting' what seemed to them not to make sense.

In 1623 John Heminges and Henry Condell, two actors in Shakespeare's company, collected together texts of thirty-six of Shakespeare's plays (*Pericles* was omitted) and published them in a large **folio** (a book in which each sheet of paper is folded once in half, to give two leaves). This, the First Folio, was followed by later editions in 1632, 1663 and 1685. Despite its appearance of authority, however, the texts in the First Folio still present many difficulties, for there are printing errors and confused passages in the plays, and its texts often differ significantly from those of the earlier quartos, when these exist.

Shakespeare's texts have, then, been through a number of intermediaries. We do not have the playwright's authority for any of his plays, and hence we cannot know exactly what it was that he wrote. Bibliographers, textual critics and editors have spent a great deal of effort on endeavouring to get behind the errors, uncertainties and contradictions in the available texts to recover the plays as Shakespeare originally wrote them. What we read is the result of these efforts. Modern texts are what editors have constructed from the available evidence: they correspond to no sixteenth- or seventeenth-century editions, and to no early performance of a Shakespeare play. Furthermore, these composite texts differ from each other, for different editors read the early texts differently and come to different conclusions. A Shakespeare text is an unstable and a contrived thing.

Often, of course, its judgements embody, if not the personal prejudices of the editor, then the cultural preferences of the time in which he or she was working. Growing awareness of this has led recent scholars to distrust the whole editorial enterprise and to repudiate the attempt to construct a 'perfect' text. Stanley Wells and Gary Taylor, the editors of the Oxford edition of *The Complete Works* (1988), point out that almost certainly the texts of Shakespeare's plays were altered in performance, and from one performance to another, so that there may never have been a single version. They note, too, that Shakespeare probably revised and rewrote some plays. They do not claim to print a definitive text of any play, but prefer what seems to them the 'more theatrical' version, and when there is a great difference between available versions, as with *King Lear*, they print two texts.

SHAKESPEARE AND THE ENGLISH RENAISSANCE

Shakespeare arrived in London at the very time that the Elizabethan period was poised to become the 'golden age' of English literature. Although Elizabeth reigned as queen from 1558 to 1603, the term 'Elizabethan' is used very loosely in a literary sense to refer to the period 1580 to 1625, when the great works of the age were produced. (Sometimes the later part of this period is distinguished as 'Jacobean', from the Latin form of the name of the king who succeeded Elizabeth, James I of England and VI of Scotland, who reigned from 1603 to 1625.) The poet Edmund Spenser heralded this new age with his **pastoral** poem *The Shepheardes Calender* (1579), and in his essay *An Apologie for Poetrie* (written about 1580, although not published until 1595) his friend Sir Philip Sidney championed the imaginative power of the 'speaking picture of poesy', famously declaring that 'Nature never set forth the earth in so rich a tapestry as divers poets have done … Her world is brazen, the poet's only deliver a golden'.

Spenser and Sidney were part of that rejuvenating movement in European culture which since the nineteenth century has been known by the term 'Renaissance'. Meaning literally 'rebirth' it denotes a revival and redirection of artistic and intellectual endeavour which began in Italy in the fourteenth century with the poetry of Petrarch. It spread gradually northwards across Europe, and is first detectable in England in the early sixteenth century in

 CHECK THE NET

You can consult texts by Spenser and Sidney, and other contemporaries of Shakespeare, at Renascence Editions **http://www. uoregon.edu/ ~rbear/ren.htm**

the writings of the scholar and statesman Sir Thomas More and in the poetry of Sir Thomas Wyatt and Henry Howard, Earl of Surrey. Its keynote was a curiosity in thought which challenged old assumptions and traditions. To the innovative spirit of the Renaissance, the preceding ages appeared dully unoriginal and conformist.

That spirit was fuelled by the rediscovery of many classical texts and the culture of Greece and Rome. This fostered a confidence in human reason and in human potential which, in every sphere, challenged old convictions. The discovery of America and its peoples (Columbus had sailed in 1492) demonstrated that the world was a larger and stranger place than had been thought. The cosmological speculation of Copernicus (later confirmed by Galileo) that the sun, not the earth, was the centre of our planetary system challenged the centuries-old belief that the earth and human beings were at the centre of the cosmos. The pragmatic political philosophy of Machiavelli seemed to cut politics free from its traditional link with morality by permitting to statesmen any means that secured the desired end. And the religious movements we know collectively as the Reformation broke with the Church of Rome and set the individual conscience, not ecclesiastical authority, at the centre of the religious life. Nothing, it seemed, was beyond questioning, nothing impossible.

Shakespeare's drama is innovative and challenging in exactly the way of the Renaissance. It examines and questions the beliefs, assumptions and politics upon which Elizabethan society was founded. And although the plays always conclude in a restoration of order and stability, many **critics** are inclined to argue that their imaginative energy goes into subverting, rather than reinforcing, traditional values. Frequently, figures of authority are undercut by some comic or parodic figure: against Prospero in *The Tempest* is set Caliban; against the Duke in *Measure for Measure*, Lucio; against Henry IV, Falstaff. Despairing, critical, dissident, disillusioned, unbalanced, rebellious, mocking voices are repeatedly to be heard in the plays, rejecting, resenting, defying the established order. They belong always to marginal, socially unacceptable figures, 'licensed', as it were, by their situations to say what would be unacceptable from socially privileged or responsible citizens.

 CHECK THE NET
The Luminarium site has links to a wide range of historical information on sixteenth-century topics including astronomy, medicine, economics and technology: **http:// www.luminarium. org**

The question is: are such characters given these views to discredit them, or were they the only ones through whom a voice could be given to radical and dissident ideas? Was Shakespeare a conservative or a revolutionary?

Renaissance culture was intensely nationalistic. With the break-up of the internationalism of the Middle Ages the evolving nation states which still mark the map of Europe began for the first time to acquire distinctive cultural identities. There was intense rivalry among them as they sought to achieve, in their own vernacular languages, a culture that could equal that of Greece and Rome. Spenser's great **allegorical** epic poem *The Faerie Queene*, which began to appear from 1590, celebrated Elizabeth and was intended to outdo the poetic achievements of France and Italy and to stand beside the works of Virgil and Homer. Shakespeare is equally preoccupied with national identity. His history plays tell an epic story that examines how modern England came into being through the conflicts of the fifteenth-century Wars of the Roses which brought the Tudors to the throne. He is fascinated, too, by the related subject of politics and the exercise of power. With the collapse of medieval feudalism and the authority of local barons, the royal court in the Renaissance came to assume a new status as the centre of power and patronage. It was here that the destiny of a country was shaped. Courts, and how to succeed in them, consequently fascinated the Renaissance; and they fascinated Shakespeare and his audience.

But the dramatic gaze is not merely admiring; through a variety of devices, a critical perspective is brought to bear. The court may be paralleled by a very different world, revealing uncomfortable similarities (for example, Henry's court and the Boar's Head tavern, ruled over by Falstaff in *Henry IV*). Its hypocrisy may be bitterly denounced (for example, in the diatribes of the mad Lear) and its self-seeking ambition represented disturbingly in the figure of a Machiavellian villain (such as Edmund in *King Lear*) or a malcontent (such as Iago in *Othello*). Shakespeare is fond of displacing the court to another context, the better to examine its assumptions and pretensions and to offer alternatives to the courtly life (for example, in the pastoral setting of the forest of Arden in *As You Like It* or

 CHECK THE BOOK

Benedict Anderson's book on the rise of the nation and nationalism, *Imagined Communities* (revised edition, 1991), has been influential for its definition of the nation as 'an imagined political community' – imagined in part through cultural productions such as Shakespeare's history plays.

Prospero's island in *The Tempest*). Courtiers are frequently figures of fun whose unmanly sophistication ('neat and trimly dressed, / Fresh as a bridegroom … perfumed like a milliner', says Hotspur of such a man in *1 Henry IV*, I.3.33–6) is contrasted with plain-speaking integrity: Oswald is set against Kent in *King Lear*.

When thinking of these matters, we should remember that stage plays were subject to censorship, and any criticism had therefore to be muted or oblique: direct criticism of the monarch or contemporary English court would not be tolerated. This has something to do with why Shakespeare's plays are always set either in the past, or abroad.

CHECK THE FILM

We can get a modern equivalent of the effect of this displacement from Christine Edzard's film of *As You Like It* (1992). Here, the court scenes are set in the luxurious headquarters of a bank or company; the woodland scenes amid a sort of 'cardboard city' of social outcasts and the vulnerable.

The nationalism of the English Renaissance was reinforced by Protestantism. Henry VIII had broken with Rome in the 1530s and in Shakespeare's time there was an independent Protestant state church. Because the Pope in Rome had excommunicated Queen Elizabeth as a heretic and relieved the English of their allegiance to the crown, there was deep suspicion of Roman Catholics as potential traitors. This was enforced by the attempted invasion of the Spanish Armada in 1588. This was a religiously inspired crusade to overthrow Elizabeth and restore England to Roman Catholic allegiance. Roman Catholicism was hence easily identified with hostility to England. Its association with disloyalty and treachery was then reinforced by the Gunpowder Plot of 1605, a Roman Catholic attempt to destroy the government of England.

Shakespeare's plays are remarkably free from direct religious sentiment, but their emphases are Protestant. Young women, for example, are destined for marriage, not for nunneries (precisely what Isabella appears to escape at the end of *Measure for Measure*); friars are dubious characters, full of schemes and deceptions, if with benign intentions, as in *Much Ado About Nothing* or *Romeo and Juliet*. (We should add that Puritans, extreme Protestants, are even less kindly treated than Roman Catholics: for example, Malvolio in *Twelfth Night*.)

The central figures of the plays are frequently individuals beset by temptation, by the lure of evil – Angelo in *Measure for Measure*,

Othello, Lear, Macbeth – and not only in tragedies: Falstaff is described as 'that old white-bearded Satan' (*1 Henry IV*, II.4.454). We follow their inner struggles. Shakespeare's heroes have the preoccupation with self and the introspective tendencies encouraged by Protestantism: his tragic heroes are haunted by their consciences, seeking their true selves, agonising over what course of action to take as they follow what can often be understood as a kind of spiritual progress towards heaven or hell.

SHAKESPEARE'S THEATRE

The theatre for which the plays were written was one of the most remarkable innovations of the Renaissance. There had been no theatres or acting companies during the medieval period. Performed on carts and in open spaces at Christian festivals, plays had been almost exclusively religious. Such professional actors as there were wandered the country putting on a variety of entertainments in the yards of inns, on makeshift stages in market squares, or anywhere else suitable. They did not perform full-length plays, but **mimes**, juggling and comedy acts. Such actors were regarded by officialdom and polite society as little better than vagabonds and layabouts.

Just before Shakespeare went to London all this began to change. A number of young men who had been to the universities of Oxford and Cambridge came to London in the 1580s and began to write plays that made use of what they had learnt about the classical drama of ancient Greece and Rome. Plays such as John Lyly's *Alexander and Campaspe* (1584), Christopher Marlowe's *Tamburlaine the Great* (about 1587) and Thomas Kyd's *The Spanish Tragedy* (1588–9) were unlike anything that had been written in English before. They were full-length plays on secular subjects, taking their **plots** from history and legend, adopting many of the devices of classical drama, and offering a range of characterisation and situation hitherto unattempted in English drama. With the exception of Lyly's prose dramas, they were composed in the unrhymed iambic **pentameters** (**blank verse**), which the Earl of Surrey had introduced into English earlier in the sixteenth century.

CHECK THE NET
Find out more about the Shakespearean theatre at **http:// www.reading.ac. uk/globe**. This web site describes the historical researches undertaken in connection with the Globe Theatre on London's Bankside, which was rebuilt in the late 1990s.

THE GLOBE THEATRE,

On the ... Bankside.

As it appeared in the reign of King James I.

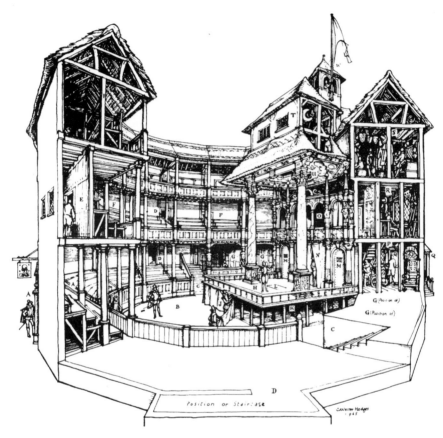

A CONJECTURAL RECONSTRUCTION OF THE INTERIOR OF THE GLOBE PLAYHOUSE

AA Main entrance
B The Yard
CC Entrances to lowest galleries
D Entrance to staircase and upper galleries
E Corridor serving the different sections of the middle gallery
F Middle gallery ('Twopenny Rooms')
G 'Gentlemen's Rooms or Lords Rooms'
H The stage
J The hanging being put up round the stage
K The 'Hell' under the stage
L The stage trap, leading down to the Hell
MM Stage doors

N Curtained 'place behind the stage'
O Gallery above the stage, used as required sometimes by musicians, sometimes by spectators, and often as part of the play
P Back-stage area (the tiring-house)
Q Tiring-house door
R Dressing-rooms
S Wardrobe and storage
T The hut housing the machine for lowering enthroned gods, etc., to the stage
U The 'Heavens'
W Hoisting the playhouse flag

CHECK THE BOOK

The most authoritative book on what we know about the theatre of Shakespeare's time is Andrew Gurr's *The Shakespearean Stage* (1992).

This was a freer and more expressive medium than the rhymed verse of medieval drama. It was the drama of these 'university wits' that Shakespeare challenged when he came to London. Greene was one of them, and we have heard how little he liked Shakespeare setting himself up as a dramatist.

The most significant change of all, however, was that these dramatists wrote for the professional theatre. In 1576 James Burbage built the first permanent theatre in England, in Shoreditch, just beyond London's northern boundary. It was called simply 'The Theatre'. Others soon followed. Thus, when Shakespeare came to London, there was a flourishing drama, theatres and companies of actors waiting for him, such as there had never been before in England. His company performed at James Burbage's Theatre until 1596, and used the Swan and Curtain until they moved into their own new theatre, the Globe, in 1599. It was burnt down in 1613 when a cannon was fired during a performance of Shakespeare's *Henry VIII*.

With the completion in 1996 of Sam Wanamaker's project to construct in London a replica of the Globe, and with productions now running there, a version of Shakespeare's theatre can be experienced at first hand. It is very different to the usual modern experience of drama. The form of the Elizabethan theatre derived from the inn yards and animal baiting rings in which actors had been accustomed to perform in the past. They were circular wooden buildings with a paved courtyard in the middle open to the sky. A rectangular stage jutted out into the middle of this yard. Some of the audience stood in the yard (or 'pit') to watch the play. They were thus on three sides of the stage, close up to it and on a level with it. These 'groundlings' paid only a penny to get in, but for wealthier spectators there were seats in three covered tiers or galleries between the inner and outer walls of the building, extending round most of the auditorium and overlooking the pit and the stage. Such a theatre could hold about three thousand spectators. The yards were about 80ft in diameter and the rectangular stage approximately 40ft by 30ft and 5ft 6in high. Shakespeare aptly called such a theatre a 'wooden O' in the prologue to *Henry V* (line 13).

The stage itself was partially covered by a roof or canopy, which projected from the wall at the rear of the stage and was supported

CONTEXT

Whereas now, we would conceptualise a visit to the theatre as going to *see* a play, the most common Elizabethan phrase was 'to go *hear* a play' (as in *The Taming of the Shrew*, Induction 2.130) – thus registering the different sensory priorities of the early modern theatre.

by two posts at the front. This protected the stage and performers from inclement weather, and to it were secured winches and other machinery for stage effects. On either side at the back of the stage was a door. These led into the dressing room (or 'tiring-house') and it was by means of these doors that actors entered and left the stage. Between these doors was a small recess or alcove which was curtained off. Such a 'discovery place' served, for example, for Juliet's bedroom when in Act IV, Scene 4 of *Romeo and Juliet* the Nurse went to the back of the stage and drew the curtain to find Juliet apparently dead on her bed. Above the discovery place was a balcony, used for the famous balcony scenes of *Romeo and Juliet* (II.2 and III.5), or for the battlements of Richard's castle when he is confronted by Bolingbroke in *Richard II* (III.3). Actors (all parts in the Elizabethan theatre were taken by boys or men) had access to the area beneath the stage; from here, in the 'cellarage', would have come the voice of the ghost of Hamlet's father (*Hamlet*, II.1.150–82).

On these stages there was very little in the way of scenery or props – there was nowhere to store them (there were no wings in this theatre) nor any way to set them up (no tabs across the stage), and, anyway, productions had to be transportable for performance at court or at noble houses. The stage was bare, which is why characters often tell us where they are: there was nothing on the stage to indicate location. It is also why location is so rarely topographical, and much more often **symbolic**. It suggests a dramatic mood or situation, rather than a place: Lear's barren heath reflects his destitute state, as the storm his emotional turmoil.

None of the plays printed in Shakespeare's lifetime marks **act** or scene divisions. These have been introduced by later editors, but they should not mislead us into supposing that there was any break in Elizabethan performances such as might happen today while the curtains are closed and the set is changed. The staging of Elizabethan plays was continuous, with the many short 'scenes' of which Shakespeare's plays are often constructed following one after another in quick succession. We have to think of a more fluid, and much faster, production than we are generally used to: in the prologues to *Romeo and Juliet* (line 12) and *Henry VIII* (line 13)

CONTEXT

We do not know much about the props list for a theatre company in Shakespeare's time, although the evidence we do have suggests that there were some quite ambitious examples: one list dating from 1598 includes decorated cloths depicting cities or the night sky, items of armour, horses' heads and 'one hell mouth', probably for performances of Christopher Marlowe's famous play *Doctor Faustus*.

Shakespeare speaks of the playing time as only two hours. It is because plays were staged continuously that exits and entrances are written in as part of the script: characters speak as they enter or leave the stage because otherwise there would be a silence while, in full view, they took up their positions. (This is also why dead bodies have to be carried off: they cannot get up and walk off.)

In 1608 Shakespeare's company, the King's Men, acquired the Blackfriars Theatre, a smaller, rectangular indoor theatre, holding about seven hundred people, with seats for all the members of the audience, facilities for elaborate stage effects and, because it was enclosed, artificial lighting. It has been suggested that the plays written for this 'private' theatre differed from those written for the Globe, since, as it cost more to go to a private theatre, the audience came from a higher social stratum and demanded the more elaborate and courtly entertainment which Shakespeare's romances provide. However, the King's Men continued to play at the Globe in the summer, using Blackfriars in the winter, and it is not certain that Shakespeare's last plays were written specifically for the Blackfriars Theatre, or first performed there.

READING SHAKESPEARE

Shakespeare's plays were written for this stage, but there is also a sense in which they were written *by* the stage. The material and physical circumstances of their production in such theatres had a profound effect upon the nature of Elizabethan plays. Unless we bear this in mind, we are likely to find them very strange, for we will read with expectations shaped by our own familiarity with modern fiction and modern drama which is, by and large, realistic; it seeks to persuade us that what we are reading or watching is really happening. This is quite foreign to Shakespeare. If we try to read him like this, we shall find ourselves irritated by the improbabilities of his plot, confused by his chronology, puzzled by locations, frustrated by unanswered questions and dissatisfied by the motivation of the **action**. The absurd ease with which disguised persons pass through Shakespeare's plays is a case in point: why does no one recognise people they know so well? There is a great deal of psychological accuracy in Shakespeare's plays, but we are far from any attempt at realism.

CHECK THE BOOK

Deborah Cartmell's *Interpreting Shakespeare on Screen* (2000) is recommended for its clear and interesting sense of the possibilities and the requirements of approaching Shakespeare through the cinema.

The reason is that in Shakespeare's theatre it was impossible to pretend that the audience was not watching a contrived performance. In a modern theatre, the audience is encouraged to forget itself as it becomes absorbed by the action on stage. The worlds of the spectators and of the actors are sharply distinguished by the lighting: in the dark auditorium the audience is passive, silent, anonymous, receptive and attentive; on the lighted stage the actors are active, vocal, demonstrative and dramatic. (The distinction is, of course, still more marked in the cinema.) There is no communication between the two worlds: for the audience to speak would be interruptive; for the actors to address the audience would be to break the illusion of the play. In the Elizabethan theatre, this distinction did not exist, and for two reasons: first, performances took place in the open air and in daylight which illuminated everyone equally; secondly, the spectators were all around the stage (and wealthier spectators actually on it), and were dressed no differently from the actors, who wore contemporary dress. In such a theatre, spectators would be as aware of each other as of the actors; they could not lose their identity in a corporate group, nor could they ever forget that they were spectators at a performance. There was no chance that they could believe 'this is really happening'.

This, then, was communal theatre, not only in the sense that it was going on in the middle of a crowd but also in the sense that the crowd joined in. Elizabethan audiences had none of our deference: they did not keep quiet, nor arrive on time, nor remain for the whole performance. They joined in, interrupted, even getting on the stage. And plays were preceded and followed by jigs and clowning. It was all much more like our experience of a pantomime, and at a pantomime we are fully aware, and are meant to be aware, that we are watching games being played with reality. The conventions of pantomime revel in their own artificiality: the fishnet tights are to signal that the handsome prince is a woman, the Dame's monstrous false breasts signal that 'she' is a man.

Something very similar is the case with Elizabethan theatre: it utilised its very theatricality. Instead of trying to persuade spectators that they are not in a theatre watching a performance,

---

CONTEXT

The Romantic critic Samuel Taylor Coleridge argued that literature requires our 'willing suspension of disbelief': but it is not clear that the theatre of the Shakespearean period did require its audience to forget that they were in a theatre. Certainly, remarks calling attention to the theatrical setting are commonplace – in comedies such as *Twelfth Night* (III.4.125) and *As You Like It* II.7.139–43, and in tragedies including *Macbeth* (V.5.23–5) – making it more difficult to forget the theatricality of the stories depicted.

Elizabethan plays acknowledge the presence of the audience. It is addressed not only by prologues, **epilogues** and choruses, but also in soliloquies. There is no realistic reason why characters should suddenly explain themselves to empty rooms, but, of course, there is no empty room. The actor is surrounded by people. Soliloquies are not addressed to the world of the play; they are for the audience's benefit. And that audience's complicity is assumed: when Prospero declares himself to be invisible, it is accepted that he is. Disguises are taken to be impenetrable, however improbable, and we are to accept impossibly contrived situations, such as barely hidden characters remaining undetected (indeed, on the Elizabethan stage there was nowhere at all they could hide).

CHECK THE NET
The 'Designing Shakespeare' database at PADS (**www.pads.ahds. ac.uk**) has an extensive collection of photographs from different productions available online.

These, then, are plays that are aware of themselves as dramas; in critical terminology, they are **self-reflexive**, commenting upon themselves as dramatic pieces and prompting the audience to think about the theatrical experience. They do this not only through their direct address to the audience but also through their fondness for the play-within-a-play (which reminds the audience that the encompassing play is also a play) and their constant use of images from, and allusions to, the theatre. They are fascinated by role-playing, by acting, appearance and reality. Things are rarely what they seem, either in comedy (for example, in *A Midsummer Night's Dream*) or tragedy (*Romeo and Juliet*). This offers one way to think about those disguises: they are thematic rather than realistic. Kent's disguise in *King Lear* reveals his true, loyal self, while Edmund, who is not disguised, hides his true self. In *As You Like It*, Rosalind is more truly herself disguised as a man than when dressed as a woman.

The effect of all this is to confuse the distinction we would make between 'real life' and 'acting'. The case of Rosalind, for example, raises searching questions about gender roles, about how far it is 'natural' to be womanly or manly: how does the stage, on which a man can play a woman playing a man (and have a man fall in love with him/her), differ from life, in which we assume the roles we think appropriate to masculine and feminine behaviour? The same is true of political roles: when a Richard II or Lear is so aware of the regal part he is performing, of the trappings and rituals of kingship, their plays raise the uncomfortable possibility that the answer to the question of what constitutes a successful king is simply: a good actor. Indeed, human life generally is repeatedly rendered through the **imagery** of the stage, from Macbeth's 'Life's but a walking shadow, a poor player / That struts and frets his hour upon the stage / And then is heard no more' (V.5.23–5) to Prospero's paralleling of human life to a performance which, like the globe (both world and theatre!), will end (IV.1.146–58). When life is a fiction, like this play, or this play is a fiction like life, what is the difference? 'All the world's a stage ...' (*As You Like It*, II.7.139).

> **CONTEXT**
>
> The poet Walter Raleigh wrote a poem on this image of life as theatre, which begins 'What is our life? A play of passion', in which 'Our mothers' wombs the tiring houses be, / Where we are dressed for this short comedy'. There's a twist at the end of the short verse: 'Only we die in earnest, that's no jest.'

CITY AND ISLINGTON
SIXTH FORM COLLEGE
283 - 309 GOSWELL ROAD
LONDON
EC1
TEL 020 7520 0652

World events

1492 Christopher Columbus sails to America

1534 Henry VIII breaks with Rome and declares himself head of the Church of England

1556 Archbishop Thomas Cranmer burnt at the stake

1558 Elizabeth I accedes to throne

1562 The English seaman, John Hawkins, first sold Africans into slavery

1568 Mary Queen of Scots taken prisoner by Elizabeth I

1570 Elizabeth I excommunicated by Pope Pius V

1571 Battle of Lepanto

1577 Francis Drake sets out on round the world voyage

1582 Outbreak of the plague in London

1584 Walter Raleigh's sailors land in Virginia

1587 Execution of Mary Queen of Scots after implicated in plot to murder Elizabeth I

1588 The Spanish Armada defeated

1589 Accession of Henry IV to French throne

1592 Plague in London closes theatres

Shakespeare's life
(dates for plays are approximate)

1564 Born in Stratford-upon-Avon

1582 Marries Anne Hathaway

1583 Daughter, Susanna, is born

1585 Twins, Hamnet and Judith, born

Late 1580s – early 1590s Probably writes *Henry VI (Parts I, II, III)* and *Richard III*

c1585–92 Moves to London

1592 Writes *The Comedy of Errors*

1593 Writes *Titus Andronicus, The Taming of the Shrew*

1594 onwards Writes exclusively for the Lord Chamberlain's Men; writes *Two Gentlemen of Verona, Love's Labour's Lost, Richard II*

1595 Writes *Romeo and Juliet, A Midsummer Night's Dream*

Literature and the arts

1513 Niccolò Machiavelli, *The Prince*

1565–7 Arthur Golding translates Ovid's *Metamorphoses*

1587 Christopher Marlowe, *Tamburlaine the Great*

World events	Shakespeare's life (*dates for plays are approximate*)	Literature and the arts
1596 Francis Drake perishes on expedition to West Indies	**1596** Hamnet dies; William granted coat of arms	
	1598 Writes *Much Ado About Nothing*	**1598** Christopher Marlowe, *Hero and Leander*
	1599 Buys share in the Globe Theatre; writes *Julius Caesar, As You Like It, Twelfth Night*	
	1600 *The Merchant of Venice* printed	
	1600–1 Writes *Hamlet, The Merry Wives of Windsor*	
	1601 Writes *Troilus and Cressida*	
	1602 Writes *All's Well That Ends Well*	
1603 Death of Queen Elizabeth I; succeeded by James VI of Scotland, who becomes James I of England	**1603** onwards His company enjoys patronage of James I as the King's Men	**1603** Michel Eyquem de Montaigne, 'Of Cannibals', translated by John Florio
	1604 *Othello* performed; writes *Measure for Measure*	
1605 Discovery of Guy Fawkes's plot to blow up the Houses of Parliament	**1605** First version of *King Lear*	**1605** Cervantes, *Don Quixote de la Mancha*
	1606 Writes *Macbeth*	
	1606–7 Probably writes *Antony and Cleopatra*	
	1607 Writes *Coriolanus, Timon of Athens*	
	1608 Writes *Pericles*; the King's Men acquire Blackfriars Theatre for winter performances	
1609 Galileo constructs first astronomical telescope	**1609** Becomes part-owner of the new Blackfriars Theatre	
1610 Henry IV of France assassinated; William Harvey discovers circulation of blood; Galileo observes Saturn for the first time		**1610** Pamphlet published entitled *A Discovery of the Bermudas, other wise called the Ile of Divels*
	1611 *Cymbeline, The Winter's Tale* and *The Tempest* performed	
1612 Last burning of heretics in England		
	1613 The Globe Theatre burns down	
	1616 Dies	
1618 Walter Raleigh executed for treason; Thirty Years War begins		
		1622 Birth of French dramatist Molière

There are many texts on Shakespeare that the interested reader might enjoy, but the following list will prove helpful.

TEXTS OF *THE TEMPEST*

The text of *The Tempest* that was published in the First **Folio** of 1623 is comparatively free from errors or problem sections and so most modern editions are based on it. This is one play, therefore, where you can choose almost any edition of the text, although the Arden, Cambridge, Heinemann, Longman and Penguin editions are particularly useful (these Notes are based on the Arden Shakespeare edition, edited by Frank Kermode). There are also recordings available if you want to hear good readings of the play, together with the use of authentic period music for the songs.

GENERAL

Catherine M. S. Alexander and Stanley Wells (eds.), *Shakespeare and Race*, Cambridge University Press, 2000
The thirteen essays in this book provide stimulating information on ethnicity, religion and politics, drawing mainly on *Othello*, *The Merchant of Venice* and *The Tempest*

Benedict Anderson, *Imagined Communities*, Verso Books, London, 1991

Charles Barber, *The English Language: A Historical Introduction*, Cambridge University Press, 2000
An excellent survey of the history and development of the English language

N. F. Blake, *The Language of Shakespeare*, Palgrave Macmillan, London, 1989

Harold Bloom (ed.), *Caliban: Major Literary Characters*, Chelsea House, New York, 1992
Caliban is one of the most intriguing characters in Shakespeare's plays and this is a stimulating study

Dwight Bolinger, *Language – The Loaded Weapon: The Use and Abuse of Language Today*, Pearson, London and New York, 1990

Michael D. Bristol, *Big-Time Shakespeare*, Routledge, London, 1997
This book evaluates the dispute concerning Shakespeare's place in the **canon** of English and European literature. Bristol is particularly useful in describing the richness of the original texts as dramatic products of a particular person at a particular time, and yet in showing how they have been interpreted – and sometimes manipulated – by subsequent generations

Deborah Cartmell, *Interpreting Shakespeare on Screen*, Palgrave, London, 2000

Samuel Taylor Coleridge, *Coleridge on Shakespeare. The Text of the Lectures of 1811–12*, edited R. A. Foakes, Routledge & Kegan Paul, London, 1971

John G. Demaray, *Shakespeare and the Spectacles of Strangeness: The Tempest and the Transformation of Renaissance Theatrical Forms*, Duquesne University Press, Pittsburg, 1998
> This is an exceptionally interesting book, but not for the faint-hearted

Michael Dobson and Stanley Wells (eds.), *The Oxford Companion to Shakespeare*, Oxford University Press, 2001
> This work describes Shakespeare's plays on the stage and on film; it covers all of his plays and poetry in short, readable entries; and includes photographs and useful references

Jonathan Dollimore and Alan Sinfield (eds.), *Political Shakespeare: New Essays in Cultural Materialism*, Cornell University Press, Ithaca, second edition, 1994
> The most interesting essay as far as this play is concerned is Paul Brown's 'This thing of darkness I acknowledge mine: *The Tempest* and the discourse of colonialism'

Howard Felperin, *Shakespearean Romance*, Princeton University Press, New Jersey, 1972
> This book examines the final plays and is useful background reading for *The Tempest*

Winifred Friedman, *Boydell's Shakespeare Gallery*, Garland, New York, 1976
> This examines some of the paintings used to represent Shakespeare's plays and characters

Gerald Graff and James Phelan (eds.), *The Tempest: A Case Study in Critical Controversy*, St. Martin's Press, New York, 2000
> This book has several good chapters that explain and challenge post-colonial readings of the play

Robert Grudin, 'Prospero's Masque and the structure of *The Tempest*' in *The South Atlantic Quarterly* 71, pp. 401–9
> This is not an easy essay but it makes some extremely interesting points about the **symbolism** of the **masque** and Caliban's role in the play

Andrew Gurr, *The Shakespearean Stage*, Cambridge University Press, 1992

Terence Hawkes (ed.), *Alternative Shakespeares*, volumes 1 and 2, Routledge, London, 1987 and 1996
> These books examine received opinions on Shakespeare and show how traditional criticism can be examined best chronologically. Volume 2 has some relevant points to make on Caliban in relation to racism and colonialism

Jonathan Hope, *The Authorship of Shakespeare's Plays: A Sociolinguistic Study*, Cambridge University Press, 1994
> Hope provides an up-to-date evaluation of techniques for judging which plays were written by Shakespeare and which might be regarded as works of collaboration

G. K. Hunter, *English Drama 1586–1642: The Age of Shakespeare*, Clarendon Press, Oxford, 1997
> This book contextualises Shakespeare in terms of Elizabethan drama generally. It provides excellent background information on audiences, performances and the dramatic possibilities of language

David Gwilym James, *The Dream of Prospero*, Clarendon Press, Oxford, 1967

David Lindley, *Court Masques: Jacobean and Caroline Entertainments, 1605–1640*, Oxford World's Classics Drama Series, Clarendon Press, Oxford, 1995
    A useful background to the origin and development of the **masque genre**; particularly good on their music

Angus McIntosh and M. A. K. Halliday (eds.), *Patterns of Language: Papers in General, Descriptive and Applied Linguistics*, Longman, Harlow, Essex, 1966
    See the chapter entitled '*As You Like It*: a grammatical clue to character'. This is a useful guide to the usage of 'thou' and 'you' in Shakespeare

Octave Mannoni, *Prospero and Caliban: The Psychology of Colonisation*, University of Michigan Press, East Lansing, 1990
    This book is old now but the reprint is well worth reading. It provides an excellent discussion of the relationship between Caliban and Prospero and the sociological implications of colonisation

Frankie Rubinstein, *A Dictionary of Shakespeare's Sexual Puns and Their Significance*, Palgrave Macmillan, London, 1995

Samuel Schoenbaum, *Shakespeare: A Documentary Life*, Oxford University Press, 1975

Alden T. Vaughan and Virginia Mason Vaughan, *Shakespeare's Caliban: A Cultural History*, Cambridge University Press, 1991
    This is well worth reading for its insights into contemporary attitudes to colonisation and indigenous peoples. The book chronicles the background against which Caliban was created and looks at how subsequent generations have regarded him

Marina Warner, *Indigo or Mapping the Waters*, Vintage, London, 1993
    Marina Warner's feminist novel is, in part, a reworking of *The Tempest*, and attempts to give a voice and a sense of history to those like Sycorax, Ariel and Caliban, who may be said to have been inadequately represented in Shakespeare's play

Michael Wood, *Shakespeare: His Life and Times*, BBC Books, London, 2003

LITERARY TERMS

Most of the unusual terms used in this book have been explained in context, but the following brief glossary may be helpful:

action in drama, action is often subdivided into external action, referring to the physical events that occur; internal action, referring to the characters' thoughts and feelings; and stage action, referring to events that actually occur on the stage

acts major divisions of a play. In Greek drama the major divisions were signalled by the participation of the chorus. Many Latin plays, including those of Seneca, were divided into five acts. Shakespeare followed this tradition

allegory the use of people, objects and events in such a way that more than one level of meaning is conveyed. Sometimes allegories are used to convey a moral or a series of moral lessons

alliteration the repetition of initial consonant sounds in stressed syllables for emphasis or decorative effect, for example: '*You nymphs, call'd Naiads*' (IV.1.128)

anachronism assignment of an attitude, event, person or thing to a place or time when such an attitude, event, person or thing did not exist

aphorism a brief, almost proverbial statement of a piece of wisdom. Gonzalo uses aphorisms almost as much as Polonius does in *Hamlet*

apron stage a stage that projects into the auditorium and cannot easily be framed by curtains

assonance the repetition of the same vowel sound. Assonance is less easy to detect in *The Tempest* than **alliteration** because the pronunciation of vowels has changed considerably over the last four hundred years. We can find an example of it in 'five' and 'lies': '*Full fadom five thy father lies*' (I.2.399)

Bible the Bible is usually considered to be composed of the thirty-nine books of the Old Testament and the Gospels, Epistles, Acts of the Apostles and Revelation of the New Testament

blank verse unrhymed verse. When the lines contain ten syllables with stresses on the second, fourth, sixth, eighth and tenth syllables, they are called iambic **pentameters**

canon see **critic**

catharsis the Aristotelian concept that tragedy can purge the emotions of members of the audience by evoking feelings of pity for the fate suffered by the protagonists and fear that similar fates might befall them

climax the turning point in the **action** of a drama

critic a person who passes judgement on the value of a piece of literature. Critics often establish a **canon**, that is, a set of literary works regarded as the best of their kind in the language

deconstruction an attempt to reveal the partially hidden meanings in a text, especially those that illuminate aspects of its relationship with its social and political context

denouement the final unravelling of the **plot**

dramatic irony when the words or actions in a play have a significance more apparent to the audience than to the character

epilogue a concluding statement

figure of speech the non-literal use of language. The most frequently used figures of speech are **metaphor** (e.g. the sun smiled) and simile (e.g. a face like the sun)

folio a printer's sheet of paper folded so as to make four pages. Shakespeare's First Folio was printed in 1623, seven years after his death

genre literature is often divided into different categories according to form or purpose. The three main categories or genres are drama, poetry and the novel

imagery the use of figurative language for imaginative and emotional reasons

madrigal a short lyric usually dealing with pastoral life or romanticised love. It varies in length between six and thirteen lines and usually has a maximum of three rhymes: '*Where the bee sucks, there suck I: / In a cowslip's bell I lie*' (V.1.88–9)

masque parades involving people wearing masks were relatively common in medieval times. This tradition was developed in the Elizabethan and Jacobean period (*c.*1580–1640) and turned into elaborate spectacles called masques, a variant spelling of 'masks'. Courtly masques were especially popular towards the end of Elizabeth's reign and during the reign of James I (1603–25). These entertainments made use of elaborate costumes and scenery and frequently involved professional musicians and dancers. The singers and dancers often wore expensive masks

metaphor a comparison where the similarity is assumed, as in I.2.318 when Prospero refers to Caliban as '*thou tortoise*' rather than saying 'you are as slow as a tortoise'

metre regulated rhythm

mime a play in which the performers use actions and gestures, rather than words, to convey their meaning

morality plays poetic drama that developed in the Middle Ages. Often abstractions such as 'peace' and 'shame' were personified. These are sometimes distinguished from miracle plays, which centred on the legends surrounding saints, and mystery plays, which were based on biblical stories

motif a recurring theme. The struggle between brothers may be regarded as a motif in *The Tempest*

nemesis divine punishment for evil deeds

pastoral literature involving a romantic view of rustic life

pentameter a line of verse containing five stressed syllables

plot a series of interrelated incidents used as the framework for a play or a piece of fiction

pun play on words that have several meanings (e.g. 'will') or that sound similar (e.g. 'grace' and 'grease')

quarto a book made up of sheets that have been folded twice so as to produce eight pages on four sheets

rhetoric the rules that underpin the creation of clear, polished and attractive structures

self-reflexive plays that comment on themselves as dramatic pieces

sub-plot a subordinate story. The actions of Trinculo and Stephano constitute a sub-plot

symbol an item or activity that has relevance on both the literal and metaphorical levels. A storm can be both literal and representative of human passions

tragicomedy a **plot** that has the elements of a tragedy but which has a happy ending

unities principles of dramatic development involving **action**, time and place

Professor Loreto Todd is a Fellow at the Academy of Irish Cultural Heritages, University of Ulster, Coleraine. She has lectured worldwide and written numerous books, including *The Language of Irish Literature*, *Modern Englishes*, *Words Apart*, *Variety in Contemporary English* and *Green English*. Her most recent novel, *A Fire in His Head*, was published in 2002. Professor Todd has been Chief Examiner for A level English and has been involved in teaching, examining and research in Africa, America and Europe. She is currently directing an international project on World English.

General editors

Martin Gray, former Head of the Department of English Studies at the University of Stirling, and of Literary Studies at the University of Luton

Professor A. N. Jeffares, Emeritus Professor of English, University of Stirling

Maya Angelou
I Know Why the Caged Bird Sings

Jane Austen
Pride and Prejudice

Alan Ayckbourn
Absent Friends

Elizabeth Barrett Browning
Selected Poems

Robert Bolt
A Man for All Seasons

Harold Brighouse
Hobson's Choice

Charlotte Brontë
Jane Eyre

Emily Brontë
Wuthering Heights

Shelagh Delaney
A Taste of Honey

Charles Dickens
David Copperfield
Great Expectations
Hard Times
Oliver Twist

Roddy Doyle
Paddy Clarke Ha Ha Ha

George Eliot
Silas Marner
The Mill on the Floss

Anne Frank
The Diary of a Young Girl

William Golding
Lord of the Flies

Oliver Goldsmith
She Stoops to Conquer

Willis Hall
The Long and the Short and the Tall

Thomas Hardy
Far from the Madding Crowd
The Mayor of Casterbridge
Tess of the d'Urbervilles
The Withered Arm and other Wessex Tales

L.P. Hartley
The Go-Between

Seamus Heaney
Selected Poems

Susan Hill
I'm the King of the Castle

Barry Hines
A Kestrel for a Knave

Louise Lawrence
Children of the Dust

Harper Lee
To Kill a Mockingbird

Laurie Lee
Cider with Rosie

Arthur Miller
The Crucible
A View from the Bridge

Robert O'Brien
Z for Zachariah

Frank O'Connor
My Oedipus Complex and Other Stories

George Orwell
Animal Farm

J.B. Priestley
An Inspector Calls
When We Are Married

Willy Russell
Educating Rita
Our Day Out

J.D. Salinger
The Catcher in the Rye

William Shakespeare
Henry IV Part I
Henry V
Julius Caesar
Macbeth
The Merchant of Venice
A Midsummer Night's Dream
Much Ado About Nothing

Romeo and Juliet
The Tempest
Twelfth Night

George Bernard Shaw
Pygmalion

Mary Shelley
Frankenstein

R.C. Sherriff
Journey's End

Rukshana Smith
Salt on the snow

John Steinbeck
Of Mice and Men

Robert Louis Stevenson
Dr Jekyll and Mr Hyde

Jonathan Swift
Gulliver's Travels

Robert Swindells
Daz 4 Zoe

Mildred D. Taylor
Roll of Thunder, Hear My Cry

Mark Twain
Huckleberry Finn

James Watson
Talking in Whispers

Edith Wharton
Ethan Frome

William Wordsworth
Selected Poems

A Choice of Poets

Mystery Stories of the Nineteenth Century including The Signalman

Nineteenth Century Short Stories

Poetry of the First World War

Six Women Poets

For the AQA Anthology:

Duffy and Armitage & Pre-1914 Poetry

Heaney and Clarke & Pre-1914 Poetry

Poems from Different Cultures

Margaret Atwood
Cat's Eye
The Handmaid's Tale

Jane Austen
Emma
Mansfield Park
Persuasion
Pride and Prejudice
Sense and Sensibility

Alan Bennett
Talking Heads

William Blake
Songs of Innocence and of Experience

Charlotte Brontë
Jane Eyre
Villette

Emily Brontë
Wuthering Heights

Angela Carter
Nights at the Circus

Geoffrey Chaucer
The Franklin's Prologue and Tale
The Merchant's Prologue and Tale
The Miller's Prologue and Tale
The Prologue to the Canterbury Tales
The Wife of Bath's Prologue and Tale

Samuel Coleridge
Selected Poems

Joseph Conrad
Heart of Darkness

Daniel Defoe
Moll Flanders

Charles Dickens
Bleak House
Great Expectations
Hard Times

Emily Dickinson
Selected Poems

John Donne
Selected Poems

Carol Ann Duffy
Selected Poems

George Eliot
Middlemarch
The Mill on the Floss

T.S. Eliot
Selected Poems
The Waste Land

F. Scott Fitzgerald
The Great Gatsby

E.M. Forster
A Passage to India

Brian Friel
Translations

Thomas Hardy
Jude the Obscure
The Mayor of Casterbridge
The Return of the Native
Selected Poems
Tess of the d'Urbervilles

Seamus Heaney
Selected Poems from 'Opened Ground'

Nathaniel Hawthorne
The Scarlet Letter

Homer
The Iliad
The Odyssey

Aldous Huxley
Brave New World

Kazuo Ishiguro
The Remains of the Day

Ben Jonson
The Alchemist

James Joyce
Dubliners

John Keats
Selected Poems

Philip Larkin
The Whitsun Weddings and Selected Poems

Christopher Marlowe
Doctor Faustus
Edward II

Arthur Miller
Death of a Salesman

John Milton
Paradise Lost Books I & II

Toni Morrison
Beloved

George Orwell
Nineteen Eighty-Four

Sylvia Plath
Selected Poems

Alexander Pope
Rape of the Lock & Selected Poems

William Shakespeare
Antony and Cleopatra
As You Like It
Hamlet
Henry IV Part I
King Lear
Macbeth
Measure for Measure
The Merchant of Venice
A Midsummer Night's Dream
Much Ado About Nothing
Othello
Richard II
Richard III
Romeo and Juliet
The Taming of the Shrew
The Tempest
Twelfth Night
The Winter's Tale

George Bernard Shaw
Saint Joan

Mary Shelley
Frankenstein

Jonathan Swift
Gulliver's Travels and A Modest Proposal

Alfred Tennyson
Selected Poems

Virgil
The Aèneid

Alice Walker
The Color Purple

Oscar Wilde
The Importance of Being Earnest

Tennessee Williams
A Streetcar Named Desire
The Glass Menagerie

Jeanette Winterson
Oranges Are Not the Only Fruit

John Webster
The Duchess of Malfi

Virginia Woolf
To the Lighthouse

William Wordsworth
The Prelude and Selected Poems

W.B. Yeats
Selected Poems

Metaphysical Poets